WOMEN'S MINISTRY ESSENTIALS

WOMEN'S MINISTRY ESSENTIALS

HOW TO BUILD AND SUSTAIN A THRIVING CHRISTIAN COMMUNITY

CYNDEE OWNBEY

BakerBooks
a division of Baker Publishing Group
Grand Rapids, Michigan

Published by Baker Books
a division of Baker Publishing Group
Grand Rapids, Michigan
BakerBooks.com

Printed in the United States of America

Library of Congress Cataloging-in-Publication Data
Names: Ownbey, Cyndee, author.
Title: Women's ministry essentials : how to build and sustain a thriving Christian community / Cyndee Ownbey.
Description: Grand Rapids, Michigan : Baker Books, a division of Baker Publishing Group, [2026] | Includes bibliographical references.
Identifiers: LCCN 2025011998 | ISBN 9781540904911 paperback | ISBN 9781540905369 casebound | ISBN 9781493452873 ebook
Subjects: LCSH: Church work with women
Classification: LCC BV4445 .O96 2026 | DDC 253.082—dc23/eng/20250916
LC record available at https://lccn.loc.gov/2025011998

Although the stories in this book are based on actual events, names have been substituted to ensure the confidentiality of the individuals and churches mentioned.

Every effort has been made to thoroughly vet the resources cited in this book. Inclusion does not equate a blanket endorsement of the author or their other works written in the past or future.

Cover design by Laura Powell

Baker Publishing Group publications use paper produced from sustainable forestry practices and postconsumer waste whenever possible.

26 27 28 29 30 31 32 7 6 5 4 3 2 1

This book is dedicated to my husband, Sean, and our boys, Nick and Cameron. Thank you for providing the spiritual support and physical labor for so many women's ministry events and activities.

Contents

A Letter to Leaders 9

Introduction 11

1. Why Women's Ministry Matters 15
2. Building a Firm Foundation for a Ministry That Lasts 33
3. Assembling and Leading a Strong Ministry Team 53
4. Discipleship Pathways: Bible Study, Mentoring, and More 78
5. Planning with Purpose: Creating a Women's Ministry Menu 107
6. Cultivating Community and Crushing Cliques 142
7. Engaging in Missions, Service Projects, and Evangelism 162
8. Communicating Clearly: Reaching the Women You Serve 178
9. Navigating Change and Addressing Sacred Cows 200

Conclusion 215

A Prayer for Leaders 217

Acknowledgments 219

Notes 221

A Letter to Leaders

Dearest women's ministry leader,

No one and no book can fully prepare you for women's ministry. The reality is no two churches and no two groups of women are the same. Yet, having served in women's ministry in five churches and in five cities, I've discovered we're more alike than we may think. Every woman needs the gospel, and every ministry needs to point women to Jesus. Leaders from churches of all sizes and all locations ask the same questions: How do we reach younger women? What can we do to get women interested in attending Bible study? How can we get more women to show up? What should we do at our women's ministry meetings?

After over twenty-five years of leading and serving women, I've noticed patterns and processes that work. It is possible to reach younger women. With a bit of work, you can get women who aren't coming to show up. I've also found it helpful to include certain key pieces in every women's ministry meeting.

I wish someone had shared these essential ingredients with me in my early days of trying to figure out how "to do" women's ministry. The few books I read were long on the why but short on the how. I needed someone who had served in the local church to tell me what actually worked. I needed a mentor who could explain how to implement and grow an effective program.

And so, in the pages that follow, I'm sharing my best women's ministry practices with you. I've packed each chapter full of my best advice, ideas, and tips. My goal is to present to you a recipe for success. Along the way, I'll provide essential ingredients and specific steps that will help your team prepare to feed your women well. I'll also share ways you can add a local flavor to your plans to serve your specific group of women.

Each chapter begins with wisdom from the Word, a verse or passage of Scripture to keep our focus in the right place, and includes a real-life ministry memory highlighting a mistake I've made or lesson I've learned. At the end of each chapter are reflection questions and a prayer to help you process what you've read and to make note of things to ponder, discuss, and pray over. Tucked between most of the chapters are additional resources. You're welcome to use these materials as is or to tweak them as needed.

I want you and your team to feel equipped and capable of providing the spiritual nourishment your women long for. The ripple effect of women living lives sold out to Jesus will change families, churches, and communities.

I can share my best tips, but it's up to you to prayerfully consider them and implement those you sense will serve your women best. Be careful not to brush aside an idea because of your church's size or history. I've learned the hard way not to put limits on what God might do and how He might do it!

You've picked up this book because God's given you a heart for the women in your church. Protect your time and relationship with the Lord, and He will keep you anchored when ministry becomes messy and you feel like giving up. As you grow spiritually through regular time in the Word and in prayer, your love for God will continue to grow and will spill over into the way you lead and serve. Your women need you to be a leader who loves God and His Word.

Whether you're trying to right the ship in your church, launch a new women's ministry program, or firm up an already solid foundation, there is something in this book for you. I pray God will direct your attention to the information you need most on the pages that follow.

May the Lord direct your steps as you seek to make Him known (Prov. 3:5–6).

For His glory,
Cyndee

Introduction

A tomboy through most of my elementary and middle school years, I never imagined that someday I'd be planning events for women in my church. Growing up as the oldest of three girls was not the world of beauty products and bows that you might imagine. No brothers meant I learned to mow the lawn and swing a hammer before I could drive. Ironically, the theater provided a respite and hiding place where I could avoid most of the typical girl drama.

Fast-forward to life as a boy mom. I quickly discovered the beauty of friendships with other women that I'd only experienced in minuscule doses before. To my surprise and great joy, bimonthly mom group meetings and weekly playdates filled my calendar. These women understood the demands of motherhood and offered sage advice when I needed it. I desperately needed community and found it.

Once the Holy Spirit opened my eyes to the need for those moms to know Jesus, I couldn't shake the desire to do something about it. My love for ministry to women blossomed as I launched and co-led a mom's group for the women in our church. There was no smooth transition from mom's ministry to women's ministry, as you'll discover later in this book.

Discouraged by the few women's ministry resources I could find online, I followed the Lord's leading to share what our church was doing and what I was learning with other leaders through my blog, *Women's Ministry Toolbox*. The need I saw for leaders to connect with each other led me to start a Facebook group where, today, over ten thousand women's ministry leaders find encouragement and support. On a daily basis, I have a front-row seat to their celebrations and struggles.

As I reflect over the emails and posts I've read from thousands of leaders, there are two things that stand out. One, leaders are lonely. No one else quite understands the weight and work of leading in women's ministry. Two, leaders are looking for other leaders to lead them. They have questions about the best ministry practices, but few answers.

I'm here to answer many of these questions. Within these pages you'll find my best advice for ministering to women, much of it learned the hard way.

What's in This Book?

Here are some of the questions I'll answer in each chapter:

Chapter 1: Why do we need women's ministry? What does the Bible say about ministry to women? What do we know about the women we're trying to reach?

Chapter 2: How do we build a solid women's ministry program? What examples do we see in Scripture that should guide our plans? How do we partner with our pastor(s)?

Chapter 3: How do we build a women's ministry team? What should we do at our team meetings? How do we craft a mission statement?

Chapter 4: What's the difference between Bible study, discipleship, and mentoring? How do we select the best Bible study for our group? How do we train our leaders? How do we know if they are making an impact?

Chapter 5: What types of events should we offer? What's the secret to a great event? How do we create our ministry calendar? Should we charge for events? How do we work within our budget?

Chapter 6: How do we cultivate community and break apart cliques? How do we make every woman feel welcome?

Chapter 7: What is the difference between missions, service projects, outreach, and evangelism? Why should we incorporate them into our ministry plans?

Chapter 8: What are the best ways to communicate with our women? What information do we need to include? How do we capture their attention?

Chapter 9: What are sacred cows, and how do we identify them? How do we make changes without making everyone mad?

Beyond providing answers to your ministry questions and tips for ministry success, this book also includes a theological basis for women's ministry in the local church. God's Word will guide our work and anchor our program offerings.

Providing Lasting Nourishment

Preparing for a women's ministry event is a lot like hosting a dinner party. There's intentional effort, thoughtful selections, and a plan for execution. Just as we shouldn't return home hungry from a dinner party, women shouldn't return home from a women's ministry event discouraged or empty. We want to provide lasting nourishment and encouragement for their souls. We want our women to feast on the Word of God. As followers of Christ, we know that only God truly satisfies. Without Him, we are empty.

In Psalm 34:8, King David invites his audience to "Taste and see that the Lord is good; blessed is the one who takes refuge in him." I love how Warren Wiersbe explains this verse: "'Taste' doesn't suggest a sip or a nibble; it implies feeding on the Lord through His Word and experiencing all He has for us. It means knowing Him better and enjoying Him more."[1] Oh, that our women would experience all that God has for them! May each one come to know Him better and enjoy Him more.

I want to help you prepare a menu of women's ministry events and activities that will satisfy the souls of your women. With a bit of prayer and preparation, you can serve up events that lead your women to Christ and allow them to taste and see that the Lord is good.

ONE

Why Women's Ministry Matters

> One generation shall commend your works to another,
> and shall declare your mighty acts.
>
> Psalm 145:4 ESV

Why women's ministry? Is it *really* needed and necessary? You picked up this book, so you probably think so, but could you make a case for women's ministry in your church if you had to? If I'm honest, for many years I knew the need, but I wasn't able to concisely articulate why Scripture supports ministry to women. In this chapter, we'll walk through three key Scriptures so you'll be able to easily make your case, if needed. We'll also look at the barriers that can keep women from participating. Some of those barriers you may already be aware of, but others might surprise you. Last, we'll take a look at the women you're trying to reach. What do you know about them? How many are single or widowed? Have you considered what generation they fall into and how that might impact what they need and what you offer?

Wisdom from the Word

Genealogies are found in almost every book of the Bible. We might be tempted to skip over these lengthy lists of unpronounceable names, but their repeated presence signals their importance. Every name is included on purpose for a purpose. Each person played a part in the story.

One of the most well-known genealogies is found in Matthew 1. Matthew purposefully begins his Gospel with Jesus's family tree, beginning with Abraham and culminating with Jesus's birth. It's a beautiful picture of prophecy fulfilled. Matthew's original audience was Jewish and would have been very familiar with the accounts from the Old Testament. As this genealogy was recited, each name would have brought to mind specific events and truths. When David's name was read, they may have recalled 2 Samuel 7:16: "Your house and your kingdom shall be made sure forever before me. Your throne shall be established forever" (ESV). Matthew wanted his audience to understand the roots of Jesus's family tree and recognize Jesus as the promised Messiah.

In biblical times, these genealogies and accounts of God's work among His people were memorized and passed from one generation to another. Parents taught their children, and their children taught their children. I'm reminded of Psalm 145:4, which says, "One generation shall commend your works to another, and shall declare your mighty acts" (ESV). Just as the Israelites shared the testimonies of God's faithfulness, so we also are called to pass down these truths to the next generation.

Our role is to share God's mighty works not just with our biological children but with all of God's children. God can use our sharing of these truths to add new names to Jesus's family tree. As you'll see throughout the pages of this book, there is great value and importance in women studying and sharing the accounts in Scripture with one another, proclaiming and praising God for the great things He has done. Sadly, this is often not happening. Women aren't reading, studying, or sharing God's Word. Many proclaim they believe the Bible but aren't necessarily reading it. A casual poll on social media asking women what they are reading in their quiet time reveals more devotional books than books of the Bible. Even women who have been attending Bible studies for years struggle to read and study the Bible on their own. We are facing a Bible literacy crisis in the church. As the culture shifts further away from biblical principles, we need our sisters in Christ to remind us of the great things God has done and to encourage us to walk in truth.

Ministry Memory

My women's ministry team had been brainstorming ideas for reaching younger women in our church for months. We wanted women of all ages to attend our events, but a glance around the room revealed they just weren't showing up. Our events had a good response, but only women ages sixty and up were represented well. The attendance at our events did not mirror the demographics in our church. Our publicity efforts were falling flat, and our reputation of being a ministry for "older" women wasn't helping. We knew our younger women would benefit, if only we could get them in the door. If only we could understand what they were looking for.

As our team batted around different ideas for reaching the younger women in our church, someone suggested connecting with the teachers of one of the young adult classes. As the women's ministry director, I was happy to make that phone call and looked forward to gathering the intel we wanted and needed. That phone conversation provided some much-needed insight. Many of our younger women were overwhelmed with the challenges of raising children, cooking meals, and shuttling children to activities (often in addition to working full- or part-time). Few had the support of local family members, and most were trying to figure these things out on their own. Adding one more thing to their calendar was viewed as a burden, not a blessing. They needed practical help, wisdom from older women, and also friendships with other women their age. With this fresh insight, our team could make some changes that would help our ministry reach every woman in our church.

Scriptural Support for Women's Ministry

Unfortunately, not everyone sees the need for a women's ministry program. For a short time, my family attended a church that did not have a structured women's ministry program. When I inquired about starting one, it was made clear that this was not, nor would it be, a part of the church's plan for ministering to women. That was hard to hear. I'd witnessed firsthand the positive impact a women's ministry program can have in a church, but the staff was not interested in my experiences. After a bit of internal grumbling and wondering why the Lord had us there, I looked for other ways I could serve women, all the while praying the Lord might change the senior pastor's mind. I wish I could report that the Lord heard and answered those prayers, but God had a different plan. He moved us into a different church community that had a healthy and established women's ministry program.

I know I'm not alone in my experience. Over the years, I've had a handful of women reach out for advice on what to do when their church staff has said no to a women's ministry program. I recently received a text from a friend who leads the women's ministry program at her church in the southwestern United States. She had attended her associational meeting the night before and reported with great sadness that of the forty-four churches in their association, only eight had a women's ministry program. While that statistic grieved my heart, I was not all that surprised.

I understand why some churches don't have or even want a women's ministry program. As you likely know, women's ministry has a reputation for offering shallow, overly feminine events and activities. I wish I could say these rumors aren't accurate, but I've seen the things some women's ministry programs promote, and the description often fits. Women's ministry in many churches is more about potlucks and parties than it is about equipping and encouraging women to live for Christ.

There may be many reasons a church staff or pastor doesn't want or see the need for a women's ministry program. Some argue that a structured program isn't needed, as the teaching of younger women by older women should be an organic outpouring of the relationships between women in the church. However, in most church communities, it doesn't happen that way. People sit with the same circle of friends in worship and in their small group. Younger women who dare to venture outside of their close-knit community to ask an older woman to disciple them are often discouraged when the older woman declines.

Some churches have discarded ministry programs to focus on a small group or community group model. Many have well-meaning church staff who believe that the purpose of small groups eliminates the need for a women's ministry program. Not true. The need remains. Small groups are just that—they're small. They may only have ten or twelve members.

They're often coed, which means out of those ten or twelve members, only five or six might be women. Small groups are also often grouped by age, and so there are rarely any older or younger women in attendance. Typically speaking, small groups are more focused on fellowship than deep Bible study. I love my small group, but it's not a place where there's a lot of cross-generational teaching between women. Small groups are good and valuable, but they cannot take the place of a healthy, vibrant women's ministry. Churches need healthy women's ministry programs to fulfill the scriptural directive that older women teach younger women.

Churches need healthy women's ministry programs to fulfill the scriptural directive that older women teach younger women.

You may need to make a biblical case for a women's ministry program in your church. Even if you don't, it is valuable to know and be able to explain Scriptures that support women's ministry. While there may not be a Bible passage that lays out a written plan for women's ministry, there *are* three specific Scripture passages in the Bible we can point to: Titus 2:3–5; Acts 2:42; and Matthew 28:19–20. Let's take a quick look at each one.

Titus 2:3–5 is probably the most cited Scripture in defense of a women's ministry program. It reads,

> Older women likewise are to be reverent in behavior, not slanderers or slaves to much wine. They are to teach what is good, and so train the young women to love their husbands and children, to be self-controlled, pure, working at home, kind, and submissive to their own husbands, that the word of God may not be reviled. (ESV)

There's a lot in that passage we could unpack, but let's fix our eyes on the end of verse 3 and the beginning of verse 4: older women are to teach what is good and train younger women. This instruction, given to the early church, still pertains today. A women's ministry program can provide opportunities for older women to teach younger women through Bible studies, discipleship groups, and events.

The second passage serves as a calendar check for us all. The early church was an active church, gathering regularly for teaching and fellowship. This is the opposite of the trend we see in churches today. According to Gallup polling, weekly church attendance has dropped from 32 percent in 2000 to 21 percent in 2023.[1] So what did early church life look like? In Acts 2:42, Paul describes the daily activities of the early church: "They devoted themselves to the apostles' teaching and to fellowship, to the breaking of bread and to prayer." In comparison, our weekly church activities fall short. We aren't gathering together with regular, daily devotion to teaching, fellowship, prayer, and breaking bread. A Christ-focused women's ministry program can bridge the gap by providing and encouraging spiritual growth.

In addition to Titus 2:3–5 and Acts 2:42, Matthew 28:19–20 provides scriptural support for women's ministry. After the resurrection, Jesus met up with the eleven disciples on a mountain in Galilee. Jesus gave them these directions: "Go and make disciples of all nations, baptizing them in the name of the Father and of the Son and of the Holy Spirit, and teaching them to obey everything I have commanded you. And surely I am with you always, to the very end of the age" (Matt. 28:19–20). Though originally given to Jesus's disciples, these instructions also apply to us today. All believers, men and women, are to make disciples. Part of the core function of women's ministry programs *should* be making disciples. Unfortunately, that's not always the case. Social functions dominate many women's ministry calendars. As we'll discuss in later chapters, it's not that we *can't* have potlucks and parties, but our purpose and activities must be grounded in Scripture.

Barriers to Participation

Crowded calendars aren't the only barrier to participation in women's ministry. Other barriers include meeting times, spiritual apathy, biblical illiteracy, and cliques. How can we increase participation?

Let's first tackle the barrier of meeting times. Historically, stay-at-home moms were the primary target audience for women's ministry in the local church. Meetings were scheduled during the daytime, and activities traditionally revolved around Bible studies and mom groups (daytime meetings that focus on fellowship and activities for moms and their children). If you've noticed dwindling numbers over the years, that's no mistake. According to the US Department of Labor, "The labor force participation rate for all mothers with children under age 18 was 71.2 percent in 2021."[2] If most of our activities are still aimed at the stay-at-home mom or only offered during the workday, no wonder attendance has dropped! Targeting traditional stay-at-home moms is no longer an effective strategy. We're reaching the minority instead of the majority.

The barrier of spiritual apathy may be more difficult to overcome. Weekly church attendance, which was once a cultural norm, is now the exception, not the rule. We exist in what has been labeled a post-Christian era. The influence of the church and Christianity is diminishing. Research reveals that while most Americans (68 percent) consider themselves to be Christian, among those self-identifying Christians only 6 percent have a biblical worldview.[3] Even those who attend regular Bible study and Sunday morning sermons often lack a solid foundation of biblical truth. Rather than view this as a crisis, we can embrace it as an opportunity and change our tactics accordingly. In the pages that follow, you'll find many ideas for reaching women who appear to be apathetic about church and religion.

Biblical illiteracy is the barrier we're most likely to dismiss. We may assume most women in our churches read the Bible regularly and use it as a guide for life. However, that's just not true. According to the 2024 "State of the Bible" report by the American Bible Society, 46 percent of self-identifying evangelicals are Scripture engaged, while just 25 percent of mainline Protestants are Scripture engaged.[4] The formula used to calculate Scripture engagement is based not only on Bible reading but on applying biblical principles. People aren't reading or applying their Bible as much as we might think. These statistics should shock us into taking action.

Cliques are another barrier to participation. Sometimes, despite our best efforts, some women feel left out at events. People tend to sit and visit with their friends, often to the exclusion of others in the room. Such "holy huddles" are commonplace, and inside jokes always leave the new girl in the dark. Even our volunteer teams draw on the same women from the same pool. Plus, our use of Christianese language (words only seasoned believers understand) leaves new believers and unbelievers on the outside.

A failure to see women as differing individuals can also stifle participation. One woman shared with me that in her church women's ministry, meetings and events were directed primarily at moms or assumed a homogeneous audience with similar interests, outlooks, culture, and calling. Sometimes our presentations and discussion questions are directed toward a core group of women, excluding those with different experiences.

All is not lost—you'll find many barrier-busting tips on the pages to come. It is possible to break up those holy huddles and increase the appetites of women for God and His Word.

A Shifting Target Audience

The composition of women in our churches today is different from what it was twenty years ago. It's not just that more women are working, as I mentioned earlier, but there are major cultural shifts we need to acknowledge. For example, women are marrying and having children later in life, if at all. Understanding such generational differences will help us better minister to the women in our church. Even if the women in our church do not exhibit the cultural characteristics shared below, they are no doubt being influenced and affected by them.

Let's look at some fast facts about the different generational groups that are most important for our conversation, then we'll follow up with some ideas on how women's ministry might be able to address some of their particular needs.

Generations Chart

Generation	Births Start	Births End	Youngest Age Today*	Oldest Age Today*
Boomers	1946	1964	61	79
Gen X	1965	1979	46	60
Millennials	1980	1994	31	45
Gen Z	1995	2012	13	30

*Ages calculated as of 2025

Gen Z

Our youngest women, Gen Z, were born between 1995 and 2012. Gen Z encompasses high school teens, young moms with children, and everyone in between. As you read through the following information, try to picture these women in your church—and their mothers who are trying to help them navigate through these sometimes challenging years.

Millennials may have been the first to master social media, but Gen Z "has never known a world without the internet."[5] Most of their social interactions are online, versus in-person. Dr. Jean Twenge, author of *Generations*, says, "This is Gen Z in a nutshell: concerned with authenticity, confronting free speech issues, pushing the norms of gender, and struggling with mental health." Twenge explains, "Not only can people be transgender, identifying with a gender different from their birth sex, but they can identify as neither male or female."[6] While we may be tempted to think this doesn't affect the women in *our* church, in 2021 one in six young adults identified as something other than straight. In a 2021–2022 survey, 23 percent of Gen Z women identified as bisexual.[7] These are stats we should not ignore.

Gen Z teens are also struggling to grow up. Author Abigail Shrier notes they are the "most fearful generation on record." When compared to Millennials, they are "far less likely to date, obtain a driver's license, hold down a job, or hang out with friends."[8] Like Millennials, they are postponing getting married and having children.[9]

Based on the information above, one might expect Gen Z women are struggling. Dr. Twenge declares, "there is a full-blown mental health crisis among young people."[10] Shrier notes that 42 percent have a mental health diagnosis.[11] It's normal not to be normal. Depression rates have risen. By 2021, nearly 30 percent of teen girls were suffering from clinical-level depression. Young people are harming themselves and committing suicide. This is not just a mental health crisis; many Gen Zers are also facing a physical health crisis. In 2019, one out of three young adults was clinically obese.[12]

What does Gen Z think about religion? Based on the information above, it may seem that they have little interest in it. However, a 2023 Barna report notes that three-quarters of US teens want to learn more about Jesus.[13] Because many Gen Zers were not raised in a Christian home, they are a "spiritual blank slate."[14] There have been documented examples of God's Spirit moving among the young people on college campuses, such as the widely reported Asbury revival in 2023. Kyle Richter and Patrick Miller report, "In the wake of the Asbury revival last spring, it looks as though the Holy Spirit is priming the souls of hundreds of thousands of teenagers and young adults for renewal—the very generation that has been repeatedly touted as the least religious ever."[15] I recently talked with a friend who serves in a Christian organization on our college campus nearby. She shared that a growing number of Gen Z students desire structured worship and deep theological teaching. They are looking for authenticity and truth.

What does Gen Z need from a women's ministry program? There is a great need for biblical discipleship and biblical counseling. Gen Z will benefit from a focus on biblical truth and biblical teaching that will help them apply the gospel to the culture. We can expect that some of the Gen Z women we interact with may struggle with same-sex attraction or their identity as a female. If they aren't wrestling with these things, their friends may be. Many of the mothers of Gen Z need support in parenting daughters (and sons) who are struggling with their sexual identity. If you don't feel prepared for these types of conversations, ask your pastor for resource recommendations and begin to build a list of books and resources you can share with these young women and their mothers. You can also offer events and Bible studies that teach biblical womanhood. Gen Z may also benefit from training in discerning feelings from truth.

There are very practical things we can do too. We need to be prepared to recommend trusted biblical counselors. We need to explain passages in the Bible and provide lyrics to worship songs, so those who grew up outside of the church can feel like part of the family. Knowing their use of technology, we should use social media to communicate with them. While these young women may appreciate beautiful things, if there's no meat at our meetings, Gen Z will go looking for it elsewhere.

If there's no meat at our meetings, Gen Z will go looking for it elsewhere.

Millennials

What do we know about the Millennial generation? The Millennial women in your church, born between 1980 and 1994, may be single, married, or divorced. They may have young or teenage children, or they may be struggling with infertility.

What sets this generation apart? They were the first to master social media. Not only did they learn how to stay in touch with friends online but the internet taught them how to start businesses, brought them news about the latest current events, and provided spaces for them to share their opinions. Millennials are the most educated generation in history. Attending college delayed adulthood and marriage for many of them. While the average age of first-time brides rose to twenty-eight, "some experts think about 1 in 5 Millennial women will never marry at all." Those who do marry become parents later in life. Cultural shifts in sexuality impacted them too. By their late twenties to mid-thirties, one in five Millennial women had at least one same-sex partner.[16]

By and large, Millennials are not happy. "Millennial adults are more likely to be depressed and more likely to die deaths of despair" (drug overdose, suicide, and liver disease). There are several reasons their mental health may be suffering. Dr. Twenge acknowledges "marriage and religion are both strong predictors of happiness," which Millennials are delaying or opting out of. Additionally, technology spreads bad news, increasing anxiety, and has decreased the amount of time people spend socializing face-to-face.[17]

What do Millennials think about religion? While many still claim to believe in God, they are the least religious generation in American history. Interestingly, Dr. Twenge believes it's because religion is not compatible with individualism, a core Millennial value. "Individualism promotes focusing on the self and finding your own way, and religion by definition promotes focusing on things larger than the self and following certain rules." Many Millennials are resistant to committing to a larger community. Some Millennials are turning to low-commitment faith substitutes such as self-care, astrology, and practicing yoga.[18]

What do older women's ministry leaders do with this information about Millennials? As we select meeting topics, plan Bible studies, and write discussion questions, we need to remember many of our younger women may be single or childless. Are we being careful not to idolize marriage or child-rearing? Are we making assumptions about the single women in our church? We might assume the single women in our church have more time for Bible study or service projects than those with families, but that isn't always true. Are we prepared to share the names of recommended biblical counselors with women who are struggling with depression or anxiety? Are we offering lots of opportunities to connect with other women face-to-face? Are we addressing the desire to focus on self? Are we acknowledging false teachings that do not align with God's Word and teaching women how to be discerning?

I share these things not to discourage you but to inform you. If we want to connect with younger women from the Millennial and Gen Z generations, we must be aware of the impact the culture has had on their lives and we must strive to understand their struggles and strengths. As you read through the pages in this book, consider how you might plan events and activities that will engage and encourage the younger women in your church and community. I hope you will see that these solutions will benefit every woman in your church, not only the younger women you may be struggling to reach.

Gen X

What sets this generation apart from the others? Generation X, or Gen X, was born between 1965 and 1979. These are the women in your church who, if they raised a family, are entering the empty nest years. They may have adult children living at home. They may split their time between caring for grandchildren and caring for their aging parents. Dr. Twenge explains they are the generation of firsts and lasts. They were the first generation to experience the internet and the last generation to play outside without supervision. Many of their childhood memories revolve around television shows.[19]

Gen X was also the first generation of children to view divorced parents as normal. One wonders how that has impacted marriage and the sexual activity of Gen X. The average age of marriage for Gen X women was twenty-five (later than previous generations). They may have been waiting to get married, but they weren't waiting to have sex. Shockingly, one out of ten Gen X teenage girls said they first had sex when they were twelve years old or younger. The support for same-sex relationships and marriage we see in Gen Z and Millennials started with Gen X. More than 50 percent of Gen X supports same-sex relationships and marriage.[20]

What does Gen X need from a women's ministry program? Often nicknamed the "sandwich generation," they may find it difficult to attend women's ministry events between caring for their adult children, their grandchildren, and their parents. Yet women will long for wisdom from those who've walked a similar path. Any tendency to focus only on young moms may leave them feeling left out. Too young for the senior citizen group and no longer connected through raising young children, if they had them, Gen X may feel there's no place for them in your church. Having graduated from the children's and youth ministries, they may quietly disappear from Sunday morning worship services. Some may travel freely now that their nest is empty, while others may be tied to an office chair, finally achieving an executive role, returning to work to help pay for college, or reentering the workforce after a divorce.

Don't be too quick to dismiss Gen Xers as uninterested. They may view that empty nest as an opportunity to focus more on God. Some Gen Xers are happy to serve in leadership positions now that they no longer have to shuttle children to activities. They may have the time to disciple younger women in your church, but they may not feel equipped to do so. You may find it helpful to offer discipleship training to bridge that gap.

Boomers

What about one of the oldest generations in your church? Boomers are those born between 1946 and 1964. Many of your Boomer women have grown up in the church. It's likely they are grandmothers and great-grandmothers. They may be widows. You might refer to them as "senior saints" or "church mothers."

The Boomer generation earned its name from the high birth rates that followed WWII. Crowded maternity wards led to crowded schools. They were the first generation to experience a world outside of their neighborhoods via television. Emotions, self-expression, and self-confidence drove this generation. Boomers were the first to read self-help books, and many became fascinated by New Age and Eastern spirituality.[21]

Their views on sexuality and marriage shifted greatly from the generation before. Most Boomers argued that sex before marriage was up to the individual. It became acceptable to stay single. When Boomers married, they waited longer to have children. Many women built their careers before they built their families.[22]

We can see the beginning of mental health decline in the Boomer generation. They were "more likely than their predecessors to be unhappy, suffer from more days of poor mental health, experience more mental distress, and be depressed."[23]

How can Boomers benefit from women's ministry? Solid biblical teaching will be key in correcting false teachings they may have picked up from self-help books, New Age, and Eastern spirituality. While they may have much wisdom to share, they may not feel confident in doing so. You may need to encourage them to mentor or disciple others. They may struggle with technology and receiving communication your ministry sends out. It may be necessary to print paper copies or invite them to events in person or via a phone call.

Boomers may enjoy participating in a senior citizen program as well as women's ministry events, so you'll want to take care to avoid any calendar conflicts. Some Boomers may not like to drive in the dark and may prefer daytime events. Transportation arrangements may be necessary for nighttime activities.

These generational descriptions are generalizations, but they can be helpful in seeing and understanding the needs of the women we serve. In the introduction of *Generations*, Dr. Twenge notes that the "era when you were born has a substantial influence on your behaviors, attitudes, values, and personality traits."[24] It's my hope that this overview of each generation will provide helpful insight into the experiences and values of the women you serve. When you select Bible studies, plan events, and write discussion questions, I hope you'll consider every woman from every generation. Will it address the questions she has? Will it meet her needs? Every event may not reach everyone, but we can try to be more inclusive of the different seasons of life our women are walking in.

What Do You Know About the Women in Your Church?

We've looked at four generations: Gen Z, Millennials, Gen X, and Boomers. How are those groups represented in your church? Which group is the biggest? Do you have more young moms or more widows? How many are college-age? How many work full-time or part-time? How many are single? How many homeschool? If your church isn't able to provide these numbers for you, I encourage you to survey as many women as possible and find out.

One team I served on asked the church secretary to pull stats of all the women at our church. We wanted to figure out what age groups were represented in our church along with how many were single, how many were widows, and how many were married. We also looked at the ages of their children. What we discovered was shocking to our team. We had no idea that we had so many older women who were widows. This immediately and greatly affected what we offered, and it even affected our discussion questions. We realized that if we were focusing our questions or events on marriage or raising children, we were leaving out a large group of women. While they could still add their experience and wisdom to the conversation, we wanted to make sure our events and discussions were more inclusive and representative of the women in our church.

How Young Is Too Young for Women's Ministry?

While we may wish to serve, support, and encourage every female in our church, regardless of her age, we need to assess if that's what's best for our women and the other ministries in our church. Titus 2 invites women to mentor younger women in the church. How can we serve the adult women in our church well while also encouraging and preparing girls to become godly women?

There are some pros and cons to inviting high school and middle school girls to women's ministry events. Inclusion does ease the transition into women's ministry events and activities. When young women already know a lot of the ladies who will be in attendance, they'll feel more comfortable attending. They know what to expect. It also allows for mentoring and discipleship opportunities. However, women's ministry activities can compete with youth ministry activities. If you are targeting high school girls, you might have to be creative and do some serious calendar coordination. You don't want young girls to have to choose between youth activities and women's ministry activities. Also, moms of teen girls might not want their daughters in attendance. The presence of teens tends to limit discussion. Some women are going to be less open about sharing personal information, and some topics are going to feel completely off-limits.

This decision should not be made in isolation. Please talk to your youth pastor and other applicable members of your church staff. Have a discussion to decide who really is your target audience. Your youth pastor may want the youth leaders to primarily serve as mentors. It may be best that certain events are open to high school girls to ease their transition into women's ministry. Every church situation is unique. While my preference is targeting women post–high school, that may not be what's best for your church. Please keep in mind that it's going to be much more difficult to adjust the target age upward if you start low. (Childcare can complicate this discussion, but we'll address that in more detail later in this book.)

Let's talk about the other end of the spectrum: There should be no age limit on participation. We need the wisdom and experience of senior saints. Don't forget to coordinate calendars with the leader of the senior adult ministry too, if applicable. Your women shouldn't have to choose between activities.

Where Is Your Target Audience Located?

It's not just age that we need to consider as we define our target audience but also physical location. We're not just targeting the women who physically and regularly attend church services. Sometimes we overlook the women in our community—the neighborhoods that surround our church building or our meeting location—and the friends of our women. While church transfer (Christians moving their membership from one church to another) is very common, that's not our goal. We want to reach women who do not know Christ and those who do not have a church home. As we plan, we need to find ways to spread the word and offer invitations to women beyond our church walls.

Physical location matters because we need to interact in person with the women we serve and support. We want to be able to take them a meal when they're in crisis. We want to be able to sit down beside them and pray with them. We also want a level of accountability. If their attendance at Bible study or church services drops suddenly, we can check in on them.

Once we have a firm grasp on why we need women's ministry and who we serve, we're ready to begin working on how we can build a firm foundation for our women's ministry program.

Reflection Questions

1. Which age group(s) do you find missing from many of your women's ministry events and activities? If it varies by event and activity, consider making a list.

2. Which generalizations about Gen Z, Millennials, Gen X, and Boomers surprised you?

3. What needs may Gen Z, Millennial, Gen X, and Boomer women have that your women's ministry could meet?

4. How would you describe your current efforts to reach unchurched women in your community?

5. Which barriers to participation do you see reflected in your church and community? List at least two examples.

6. What did you find most encouraging or challenging in this chapter?

Praying Through the Process

Lord, help us open our eyes to see the women in our church and community as they are. Help us be more aware of their spiritual lives. Loosen our grip on how we've carried out women's ministry events in the past and show us how we specifically need to adjust our ministry plans to better reach the women You've placed in our path. Amen.

TWO

Building a Firm Foundation for a Ministry That Lasts

> Unless the Lord builds the house,
> the builders labor in vain.
>
> Psalm 127:1

It might be tempting to fill your ministry calendar with a bunch of different events and activities you've found online or gathered from a survey of the women in your church. It can feel a bit like throwing spaghetti at a wall to see what sticks. Some may be very successful, but others may not be so much. What if, instead, we stopped to look at the examples we see in Scripture? Are there women in the Bible who can show us what ingredients we need to combine to create an event that would invite women to taste and see that the Lord is good? Is there a secret ministry recipe for success? I think so. In this chapter, I'll share five keys to a firm women's ministry foundation. We'll blanket those plans with prayer and add additional strength with pastoral support.

If you're starting or restarting a women's ministry program in your church, please do not neglect this chapter. And if you're leading in an established women's ministry program, now's a great time to assess your foundation and make the necessary repairs. Your ministry will be better when its foundation is firm.

Wisdom from the Word

Tucked inside the pages of the book of Matthew is a message about the importance of building our lives on the solid foundation of Christ. Jesus wraps up the Sermon on the Mount with a parable about two houses. It's just three short verses (Matt. 7:24–27), but the image and lesson are powerful. The first house is built on the rock: When "the rain came down, the streams rose, and the winds blew and beat against that house . . . it did not fall, because it had its foundation on the rock" (v. 25). The other house, built on sand, is unable to withstand the storm: "The rain came down, the streams rose, and the winds blew and beat against that house, and it fell with a great crash" (v. 27).

It seems fairly straightforward: Don't build your house on the sand. I live in North Carolina, where the coast is dotted with houses built on the sand. Hurricanes regularly strike our beautiful beaches and threaten to tear those houses down. Thankfully, most have been built on a solid foundation and easily weather the storms. On many of our trips to the beach, we've had the opportunity to see the foundation for a beach house being built. The builder drives more than a dozen pilings (long, heavy wooden beams) down through the sand into the solid ground. These pilings provide solid footings for the house that will be built on top. The house looks like it's sitting on top of shaky stilts, but it's solid and elevated to protect it from flooding. It's a noisy and lengthy process, as each piling is beaten down farther and farther into the sand until it's secure. It's also time-consuming and costly, but it's necessary for withstanding the storm.

Jesus rightly calls the man who built his house on the rock "wise" and the man who built his house on the sand "foolish." The risk of the house collapsing on the sand or being washed away in the water is high without pilings anchoring it into the ground. The application is simple: Christ must be our firm foundation. A life or a ministry built on anything else will crumble and fall.

We can expect that storms in ministry will threaten to topple our efforts. Wise leaders will take the necessary steps and time to build (or rebuild) a firm ministry foundation. Whether you've inherited a women's ministry team or are seeking to build a new one, establishing a firm foundation benefits everyone—you, your women, and your church.

Ministry Memory

During the seven years prior to my entrance into women's ministry, I served in two secular groups for moms. I joined my first moms' group when our oldest son, Nick, was just four months old. Nick was due to arrive just as I should have been wishing my first graders a happy summer, but he arrived three weeks early. I was dropping off lesson plans, adjusting to being a new mom, and waiting for our new house, the first to be finished in our new neighborhood, to pass its final inspection. It was a lonely time. I was no longer working and we had virtually no neighbors. Living far from family and without a budget to support numerous long-distance phone calls, I found that mom group to be an answer to my prayers. I was desperate for community and encouragement. I soon found it to also be a place where I could use my teaching skills to plan social events and lead meetings. With each passing year, friendships deepened. It was such a sweet season. Then I fully surrendered my life to Christ.

As I hinted in the introduction, my longing to point moms to the real hope and help that can only be found in Jesus led me to leave my secular community group to launch and co-lead a Christian moms' group in our church. Though my heart's desire was to boldly share Jesus, we leaned heavily into the lifestyle evangelism described in our leadership materials, softening our approach so as not to offend anyone. They were the experts. They knew best, right? Our focus was on showing each mom God's love through our actions, but not with a lot of words. The few prayers we prayed at our meetings were purposefully shallow. Instead of infusing our meetings with biblical truth and the gospel, we saved that for one "special" meeting each semester. Ironically, our well-meaning desire for women to see Jesus through us only pointed women to our good works and not to Christ's offer of salvation. The lack of spiritual depth at our bimonthly meetings hinted at the poor foundation on which we had attempted to build this new ministry. It should have been no surprise when the increasing fractures in our team led to a collapse by the first year's end.

If only we had taken the time to build our new ministry on the rock-solid foundation of God's Word. God doesn't tell us to hide our faith under a bushel as we had done. Matthew 5:15 says, "Neither do people light a lamp and put it under a bowl. Instead they put it on its stand, and it gives light to everyone in the house." Neither does He instruct us to only share the good news at predetermined times. First Peter 3:15 says, "Always be prepared to give an answer to everyone who asks you to give the reason for the hope that you have." We knew where and how these moms could find true hope and peace, and we should have shared that knowledge at every chance we had. It still grieves my heart that we didn't.

What does it look like to build a women's ministry program on the rock instead of the sand? In this next section, we'll look at essential pillars for women's ministry.

Five Pillars

Early in our marriage, I discovered my husband and I had different dinner expectations. My mother-in-law always served her family meat with a vegetable and at least one starchy carb. I was raised differently. In our family, it wasn't unheard of to have popcorn for dinner on Sunday nights, and meat was not a requirement for the main dish. I was completely unaware of the "blunder" I made by serving macaroni and cheese as the main course. After we sat down to eat, my husband asked, "Where's the meat?" He actually got up to check the oven, as if I'd forgotten to take it out. After a bit of back and forth, I finally realized that in his family macaroni and cheese was only served as a side dish. If memory serves, he heated up a couple of hot dogs that night to eat alongside his macaroni and cheese.

Just as my husband would think a meal without meat is incomplete, there are essential ingredients that help create a balanced, biblical women's ministry event. These ingredients are what make a women's ministry event different from a neighborhood get-together or a social event like a baby shower or birthday party. What are these essential ingredients? They are the things that make Christians different: prayer, care, theology, evangelism, and discipleship. Like the pilings that add strength and stability to a house built on the beach, each of these essential ingredients (or pillars) adds strength to the foundation of your women's ministry program and ensures it will weather the storms when they come.

Let's take a look at the women in the Bible who were known as prayer warriors, caregivers, theologians, evangelists, and disciple-makers. There is much we can learn from them and apply to the foundation of our women's ministry programs.

Prayer

Hannah, one of many female prayer warriors in the Bible, was one of two wives of Elkanah. Peninnah, the other wife, had many children, but Hannah had none. Year after year, the Lord kept Hannah's womb closed, and Peninnah provoked her. First Samuel 1:10 says, "In her deep anguish Hannah prayed to the LORD, weeping bitterly." She made a vow to the Lord that if He were to give her a son, she would give the child to Him. Eli, the priest, observed Hannah weeping and praying. Her lips were moving, but no sound was coming out. She was carrying on in such a way that Eli thought she was drunk. Hannah explained she was not drunk; she was pouring her soul out to the Lord (v. 15). The Lord answered Hannah's prayers and blessed her with a son. "She named him Samuel, saying, 'Because I asked the LORD for him'" (v. 20).

Once Samuel was weaned, Hannah and her husband followed through on her promise and took him to the house of the Lord. In 1 Samuel 2 we see her beautiful prayer of thanksgiving, which begins with these words: "My heart rejoices in the LORD; in the LORD my horn is lifted high. My mouth boasts over my enemies, for I delight in your deliverance" (v. 1). Hannah prayed bold, consistent prayers. She was not afraid to ask God to change her circumstances and grant her request. When God answered, Hannah's response was prayer and praise.

In Luke 2:36–38 we find another prayer warrior celebrating the birth of a baby—and this was not any baby; this was baby Jesus. Anna, a prophetess, was widowed after only seven years of marriage. She devoted the rest of her eighty-four years to prayer as she awaited the arrival of the Messiah. "She never left the temple but worshiped night and day, fasting and praying" (v. 37). When Joseph and Mary brought Jesus to the temple in Jerusalem to present Jesus to the Lord, Anna immediately recognized Jesus as the promised Messiah. She approached them and "gave thanks to God and spoke about the child to all who were looking forward to the redemption of Jerusalem" (v. 38). Anna was a patient, committed prayer warrior. She fasted and she worshiped night and day.

Finally, let's look at Acts 16:13. Paul, Timothy, and their companions were traveling from town to town, encouraging churches and preaching the Word, and they made a stop in Philippi. Acts 16:13 says, "On the Sabbath we went outside the city gate to the river, where we expected to find a place of prayer. We sat down and began to speak to the women who had gathered there." Did you catch that they *expected* to find a place of prayer? Word had gotten around that a group of praying women could be found outside the city gate at the river. Paul didn't stumble upon this group of prayer warriors; he sought them out. Do you know of a group of women in your church who meet regularly to pray? If not, perhaps this is something you may want to pray the Lord would lay upon the hearts of the women in your church.

Not long ago, I was blessed to hear about a ladies' prayer ministry at a small church on the outskirts of Indianapolis. Every Sunday morning, from 7:00–7:30, they get on a call and pray. They cover the monthly prayer list, they pray for the church service, and they lift up any other requests. There's no strict, formal structure. One at a time, as women feel led, they share a short prayer.

Prayer is an essential ingredient for women's ministry. It should guide every decision your ministry makes and cover the preparations and registrations for every event. Women should recognize your ministry as a place where they can find and receive prayer support. Your events should incorporate prayer by opening and closing the event with prayer. You might include time at the end of table discussions for women to share prayer requests. Your Bible study, small group, and discipleship leaders should facilitate collecting and sharing prayer requests at each weekly meeting. Just like the group of women at the river, we should have a desire to be known as women who pray.

Care

Our second essential ingredient is care. Who are some of the women in the Bible known for being compassionate caregivers? Let's start by looking at Tabitha in the book of Acts. Tabitha, also known by her Greek name, Dorcas, was a disciple who "was always doing good and helping the poor" (Acts 9:36). When Tabitha became sick and died, her friends sent for the apostle Peter. Through Peter, the Lord raised Tabitha from the dead. News of this miracle spread all over Joppa, and many people believed in the Lord (v. 42). While nothing else is recorded about Tabitha, her character traits are forever recorded in Scripture. God wanted it known that she cared well for others.

We find the account of another caregiver, Lydia, in Acts 16. Lydia was one of the women Paul and his companions met at the prayer gathering by the river. "The Lord opened [Lydia's] heart to respond to Paul's message. When she and the members of her household were baptized, she invited us to her home" (16:14–15). She did not just open her home once to Paul and his traveling companions; when he and Silas were released from prison (v. 40), they returned to Lydia's home. We can assume Lydia was a gracious hostess who made Paul feel welcomed and cared for.

For our last caregiver example, we'll reflect upon the life of the Proverbs 31 woman. God provides a detailed description of her in Proverbs 31:10–31. While scholars debate whether or not this was a real person or meant to be a list of qualities to look for in a wife, either way, her example of caregiving is one we can strive for. The Proverbs 31 woman "works with eager hands" (v. 13), "she provides food for her family" (v. 15), and "she sets about her work vigorously" (v. 17). In verse 20, we see, "She opens her arms to the poor and extends her hands to the needy." She "supplies the merchants with sashes" (v. 24) all while "she watches over the affairs of her household" (v. 27). Verse 31 is a call to "Honor her for all that her hands have done, and let her works bring her praise at the city gate." All of these are the activities of a caregiver who not only cares for her family but also the people in her community.

Some time ago, one of the leaders in my Facebook group asked for examples of a widows' ministry. Several leaders from a variety of churches quickly responded with the details about their widows' ministry. One leader explained they had a widow and senior ministry for women called Carpenter's Daughters, through which they hosted a potluck on the first Monday of every month and ministered to each other in a very tender way. They also had a dedicated staff person who maintained a text thread for younger widows, who had different needs than the older widows. Another leader shared that their widows met in the morning twice a month for a time of fellowship and a message. They also met once a quarter for dinner. She noted their widows had found the emotional support to be incredibly valuable. As most of their widows were more apt to talk to friends about issues than ask for assistance outright, when a need was identified (such as yard work or house or car repairs), the leader coordinated with their men's service team to take care of the issue. Your church might not need a widows' ministry, but you may have need for a different kind of care ministry.

Care and compassion are critical to a solid women's ministry foundation. The love and care we show for those in and outside of our church community reflect our love for Jesus. As we make ministry plans, care and compassion should guide us. While we won't be able to meet every individual need or preference, we can be thoughtful in the decisions and plans we make. I've been reminded by team members who are gifted in decorating that small touches, such as table decorations, can make women feel loved. The preparations we make before our women arrive communicate that we care. We show women we care when we warmly welcome them when they enter the event space. Additionally, your ministry might plan service projects to love the less fortunate in your community or plan a time to assemble and distribute care packages. Like the churches mentioned above, your ministry might support a widows' ministry under the umbrella of women's ministry.

Theology

Theology, the study of God, is the third essential ingredient every women's ministry needs. Our Bibles allow us to study God so we can understand His character. Who are the women in the Bible that give us an example of studying God?

In Luke 10:38–42, Jesus and His disciples "came to a village where a woman named Martha opened her home to [them]" (v. 38). Martha's sister, Mary, "sat at the Lord's feet listening to what he said" (v. 39). Martha was left to do all of the preparations by herself; frustrated, she demanded that Jesus tell Mary to get up and help. Much to Martha's surprise, Jesus responded, "Mary has chosen what is better, and it will not be taken away from her" (v. 42). Jesus did not discourage Mary from being His student; in fact, He encouraged it!

Priscilla is another student of God and His Word. The apostle Paul stayed with and worked alongside tentmakers Priscilla and Aquila, her husband (Acts 18:2–3). Priscilla and Aquila were more than just tentmakers; they were also theologians. Later in verse 26, we read that they spent time privately with Apollos, a teacher in the synagogue, helping him teach more accurately. To correct others would require Priscilla to have a solid understanding of God and His Word.

To share God's Word with the women in our churches, we must have a solid understanding of it for ourselves. While strong Bible knowledge shouldn't be a requirement for every woman on your team, growth in their knowledge of God's Word should be a goal for every team member. How will your team help other women grow in their knowledge of God and His Word? Will you offer weekly Bible studies? Will you offer discipleship groups for those who want to go deeper? Will you seek out teachers for your events and retreats who are spiritually mature and gifted in teaching through a Scripture passage? Perhaps you'll select a Scripture focus for the year, and each event you offer will help women understand God's Word in a deeper or different way.

The women's ministry at the previous church my family attended had a strong history of focusing on God's Word. Each year their women's ministry leader prayerfully selected a biblical theme or Scripture passage that would be unpacked at events throughout the year. The women in the church were invited to memorize the focal Scripture passage. At their annual fall retreat, the speaker would teach on related passages, helping women to grow in their knowledge of God's Word. Event by event, they added new layers of understanding, encouraging all participants to be theologians.

Evangelism

Evangelism is the fourth essential ingredient for women's ministry. The *Holman Illustrated Bible Dictionary* defines evangelism as the "active calling of people to respond to the message of grace and commit oneself to God in Jesus Christ."[1] If women are going to taste and see that the Lord is good, they must first become a follower of Christ. Anyone who is a follower of Christ can, and should, share the good news. If you've found hope and freedom in Christ Jesus, you want others to have that too.

I love the examples we have in Scripture of women who were bold to share the gospel. In John 4, Jesus intentionally went through the region of Samaria on His way to Judea. He sat at the well and waited for the unnamed person we refer to today as the Samaritan woman. Jesus asked her for a drink, but He had really come to offer her living water. Jesus then asked her to call her husband (v. 16), but she admitted she had no husband. Jesus acknowledged she'd had five husbands and the man she was with now was not her husband. At first, the woman just saw Jesus as a prophet (v. 19), but then her eyes were opened to the truth when Jesus revealed His true identity. When the disciples came back and disrupted their conversation, the woman left. She went to the people in her town and told them, "Come, see a man who told me everything I ever did. Could this be the Messiah?" (v. 29). As a result of this Samaritan woman sharing the good news, "Many of the Samaritans from that town believed in him because of the woman's testimony, 'He told me everything I ever did'" (v. 39). Because she shared this good news with others, they also believed.

A second example of women evangelizing can be found in the four Gospels. Matthew 28:1–8; Mark 16:1–8; Luke 24:1–9; and John 20:1–2 all contain accounts of women visiting Jesus's grave and finding it empty. While the records of the event vary slightly and note different women in attendance, in three of the accounts an angel gives the women instructions to go and tell. "Go and tell" is the heart of evangelism. Anyone who has personally experienced Jesus, as these women did, is to go and tell others about Him.

We have a responsibility to tell others the good news. Romans 10:14–15 says,

> How, then, can they call on the one they have not believed in? And how can they believe in the one of whom they have not heard? And how can they hear without someone preaching to them? And how can anyone preach unless they are sent? As it is written: "How beautiful are the feet of those who bring good news!"

Our women need to hear the good news. They can't believe if they haven't heard. You may be the first one to tell them.

If sharing Christ is something new to you or makes you anxious, you might be tempted to let others do it. I get it. The first time I was tasked to share the gospel, I punted. I was the women's ministry director and by default the emcee for our annual fall retreat. Our speaker, a wonderful woman in our church, and I had talked about who would share the gospel during our last session on Sunday morning. I assured her that I would be happy to do so. But when it came time, I struggled to find the right words. Instead of sharing how Jesus died to save us from our sins, I simply said, "If you have any questions about how you can know Jesus as your personal Savior, please talk with our speaker or one of our team members." The women in attendance probably had no idea that I took the easy way out, but I felt awful about it. God had given me the opportunity to tell others how they could know Him personally, and I didn't take it. The regret and shame I felt kept me from making the same mistake twice.

What could evangelism look like in your women's ministry program? It may be as simple as including a time where you share the gospel at your events. We might assume every woman at our events has a personal relationship with Jesus, but that's rarely the case. I grew up attending a church that didn't preach about salvation. I wasn't taught that I needed to acknowledge my sin or that I needed a Savior who died for my sins. No one explained that the gifts of salvation and eternal life were mine if I would confess, repent, and accept Jesus as Lord of my life.

Evangelism in your ministry can also include training women to share the good news. Your church may have an evangelism technique someone on staff could share with your women. Perhaps you could teach your women how to share the gospel message, and then provide time for them to practice with one another. Maybe then they won't punt like I did. Or perhaps you'll want to schedule an evangelism training for your women's ministry team and Bible study leaders so each feels confident in sharing the gospel and praying with someone who wants to accept Christ as their Savior. Evangelism can also involve going out from your ministry and into communities to share the gospel.

Discipleship

Our fifth and final essential ingredient of women's ministry is discipleship. Discipleship is closely connected to theology; it is taking the knowledge one has learned about God (theology) and putting it into action.

Discipleship is about becoming like Jesus. James, the half brother of Jesus, understood that works are the fruit of our faith. James 1:22 says, "Do not merely listen to the word, and so deceive yourselves. Do what it says." Do the women in your church exhibit the fruit of their faith? Emphasizing discipleship in our ministry offerings can encourage women to obey the Word of God. Put simply, our role as leaders is to encourage our women to become more like Jesus.

Who are the scriptural examples of female disciple-makers? We've already mentioned one, Priscilla. While Scripture only notes that Priscilla and her husband, Aquila, discipled Apollos, 1 Corinthians 16:19 also tells us that a church met at Priscilla and Aquila's house. Good church leaders want their members to know what God's Word says and to live according to it. We can assume Priscilla actively discipled the other members in their church.

Another biblical example of disciple-makers is Lois and Eunice. Are those names familiar to you? Paul, in a letter to Timothy, encouraged him to remain faithful, saying, "I am reminded of your sincere faith, which first lived in your grandmother Lois and in your mother Eunice and, I am persuaded, now lives in you also" (2 Tim. 1:5). Paul recognized the role Timothy's mother and grandmother had in his faith. We can assume they spent years teaching Timothy what the Scriptures said and encouraging him to obey them. Just as Lois and Eunice discipled Timothy, older women in our church can disciple younger women in the faith.

That brings to mind the three key verses supporting ministry to women we discussed in the previous chapter. You may remember, we looked at Titus 2:3–5, which commands older women to teach younger women. That is discipleship. We looked at Acts 2:42, which reports that the early church was devoted to teaching. Teaching women about God and His Word is discipleship. Finally, we looked at Matthew 28:19–20, which couldn't be more clear. Jesus tells His followers to "go and make disciples." Discipleship is essential. We can't have an effective women's ministry program without it.

What could discipleship look like in your church? That's a big question with a long answer. For example, it could involve organizing Bible studies for groups of women in your church, or it might look like smaller groups of women meeting weekly for accountability and studying God's Word. In chapter 4, we'll dive deeper into the topic of discipleship.

Imagine, for a moment, the strength of a women's ministry program built on the five essential pillars of prayer, care, theology, evangelism, and discipleship. Can you see how a ministry event that incorporates all five ingredients could help women become more like Christ? I want to challenge you to refer back to these five essential ingredients as you pray and as you plan. Let them influence your mission statement, the types of events you place on your ministry calendar, and your prayers for your women. Much like the pilings on a beach house, a women's ministry program built on these five essential pillars will be strong enough to weather the storms that may threaten it.

Forming a Solid Foundation

How do we go about building this solid women's ministry foundation? Just as bricks need mortar to hold them together, a wise leader will use prayer and pastoral support to bind the foundation of their ministry.

I regularly receive messages from women's ministry leaders who are struggling to fix ministry mistakes that could have easily been prevented. Some leaders placed every interested woman on the women's ministry team. Others have awakened to the realization that their women have little desire for God or His Word. The root cause is almost always the same: Their ministry was not built on a firm foundation, and they've failed to use the tools God has given them. It's never too late to build or rebuild the foundation of your women's ministry program.

Prayer

The very first time I stepped into women's ministry, it was to take on the position of women's ministry director that had been empty for a year and a half. The prayer group I was in prayed weekly for the needs of our church, and we'd been lifting up this specific need for months. Week after week, this need in our church burdened my soul. Each week I would pray, "Lord, please send someone to lead our women's ministry team. I know it's not me." Or so I thought. Then one day as I was reading my Bible, God grabbed my attention as I read 1 Timothy 1:12: "I thank Christ Jesus our Lord, who has given me strength, that he considered me trustworthy, appointing me to his service." Despite my lack of experience and spiritual immaturity, I recognized this was a nudge from the Holy Spirit. I was young both physically (a mom with two boys in elementary school) and spiritually (I had only accepted Christ as my Savior about six years prior), and yet I chose obedience over fear. When I shared this revelation with my prayer group, they admitted they had known for weeks God was calling me to serve as the women's ministry director.

Before you speak to a staff member, assemble a team, or even begin to plan your first event, prayer is a necessity. I don't know how long God will have you on your knees, but I trust the Holy Spirit will give you a nudge when it's time to move forward.

If you are not sure what to pray while you wait for a green light from God, here are some suggestions:

1. Pray for the softening of the hearts of the women in your church and community.
2. Pray God will stir up a desire for women to be in His Word.
3. Pray for the church staff to be receptive and supportive.
4. Pray for budgeted funds to be made available (though don't make that a requirement—you can run a women's ministry on a zero budget).
5. Pray for God to put women in your path who have a heart for ministering to other women.
6. Pray God will grow and refine your leadership skills.
7. Pray for opportunities to learn from other leaders.
8. Pray for one or more verses of Scripture that can serve as the focus of your women's ministry.
9. Pray for any logistical needs.
10. Pray for the meeting you'll schedule with your pastor(s).

I love the word picture God provides in Psalm 119:105: "Your word is a lamp for my feet, a light on my path." It's a lamp, not a flashlight. God will give you enough light to see just far enough ahead to take the next step. If we could see the whole path before us and the dangers, distractions, and opposition we were going to face, we'd be tempted to run away in fear or strike out on our own path and miss what God has planned. Keep moving forward, one step at a time, praying and trusting God will show you what to do next.

Pastoral Support

Prayer without pastoral support will result in a shaky ministry foundation. Your women's ministry program should function as an arm of your local church. It's critical that you receive approval from the pastor and staff at your church. The Bible is very clear about our responsibility to submit to the authorities God has put in place (1 Cor. 1:10; Heb. 13:17). Our role is always to complement and not compete with other church ministries and events. Launching with their support helps to build a firm foundation.

When you schedule that first meeting to speak with your pastor to start (or restart) your women's ministry program:

1. Make an appointment. Do not show up unannounced or catch them in the hallway.
2. Present a clear and concise plan.
3. Explain why there is a need for a women's ministry. Highlight gaps in what is currently being offered, without being negative or rude.
4. Detail how you plan to meet the needs of the women in the church.
5. Share why and how God has led you to this point.
6. Tell them about other women who have been praying and/or the names of those you would like to be approved as members of the women's ministry team. Be specific about the roles in which they would serve. (You'll find more information on how to recruit your team members later in the next chapter.)
7. Take care not to become overly emotional. Share facts and numbers that support your plan.

8. Ask for their advice. Get their input.
9. Ask if they have questions. Be honest; if you don't know the answer, say so.
10. Invite them to pray about it and speak with other staff members before letting you know if you can proceed.

I wish this weren't true, but your pastor may say no. As I mentioned earlier, for a short time my family attended a church that did not have a women's ministry program. While I never met with the pastor, other staff members *repeatedly* made it clear that a women's ministry was not and would not be part of that church's plan or offerings. It grieved my heart, as I could clearly see the need and knew women in the church were desperate for a women's ministry. I prayed and waited for God to change their hearts.

If your church leadership says no, spend more time in prayer, continuing to seek God's will. He may eventually change the hearts of those in authority or even physically move someone new into a position of authority that will be open to the addition of a women's ministry. While you wait on God to open doors, serve your women the best that you can in the ways that *are* available. God's timing is perfect. Trust He is working in the waiting.

Meeting with Your Pastor

I used to dread meeting with the pastor who oversaw the women's ministry team. I was afraid of saying the wrong thing, not having the right answers, and presenting an idea and getting a big fat no. Instead of having a meeting scheduled, it was either up to me to reach out when an issue came up or I would be summoned to the pastor's office if there was a concern. No wonder I was a nervous wreck! Had we met regularly, it would have significantly reduced my stress level, and our women's ministry would have benefited.

Meeting when needed is a good thing, but there is also value in meeting consistently. Meeting regularly (monthly, bimonthly, or quarterly) with your pastor ensures you are working together to further God's kingdom and encourage the spiritual growth of your women. If the church staff or your pastor does not believe that the women's ministry is supporting the church's mission, the future of women's ministry could be in trouble!

Meeting with your pastor regularly:

- *Is biblical.* Hebrews 13:17 makes it clear we are to submit to our leaders in the church: "Have confidence in your leaders and submit to their authority, because they keep watch over you as those who must give an account. Do this so that their work will be a joy, not a burden, for that would be of no benefit to you."
- *Offers protection when conflict arises.* Not only can your pastor provide wise, biblical counsel, but when accusations are made or rumors fly, a good working relationship benefits everyone. If your pastor is already aware of the situation, they may be able to respond immediately. You want your pastor to say with confidence when a problem comes across their desk, "That doesn't sound like Patricia. Let me talk with her, and I'll get right back to you."
- *Allows you to share specific prayer requests and praises.* Share what God is doing through the women's ministry. Offer a few stats and stories. Your pastor can't pray specifically for the women's ministry if they don't have the details. We all need as much prayer coverage as we can get! Ask your pastor to share your requests with the rest of the church staff when applicable.

Even if your pastor trusts you and your team to minister to women without regular meetings, the team leader or co-leaders should try to schedule short thirty-minute meetings quarterly. You may need to make an official request to meet with your pastor. Explain why you'd like to meet and mention some of the benefits listed above. Hopefully, they won't need to be convinced that meeting regularly benefits everyone. If you are an unpaid volunteer, like most leaders, there may be no precedent for meeting with the pastor who oversees the women's ministry program. Ask the Lord to help you word your meeting request. Start by requesting just one meeting and go from there.

Quick tips for meetings with your pastor:

- Keep it brief. Make notes about what you want to discuss.
- Consider providing questions in advance so they can be prepared to answer them.
- Keep your emotions in check.

- Share more stats and facts than stories.
- Be gracious and grateful.
- Accept the answer and process it later.
- Thank them for their time.

If your pastor is unwilling to meet, pray over the situation and send them brief status updates quarterly. God may change their heart and mind in time.

Reflection Questions

1. How would you describe the foundation of your women's ministry program?

2. If you have an established women's ministry, which essential ingredient (prayer, care, theology, evangelism, discipleship) does your team need to be more intentional about including?

3. Does your foundation need to be strengthened by including regular times of prayer or regular meetings with your pastor? If so, how will you take action to implement what is lacking?

4. What did you find most encouraging or challenging in this chapter?

Praying Through the Process

Father, our ministry is only as strong as its foundation. Please help us to see any cracks in it. Help us to strengthen our foundation with the essential ingredients of prayer, care, theology, evangelism, and discipleship. Help us to be faithful to pray for the women in our church and our ministry plans. Help us to communicate well with our pastor(s) so they can pray for and support our women's ministry program. We cannot do this without You and without the support of others. Amen.

Twenty-One Scriptures to Pray for Your Women

1. Be devoted to prayer (Col. 4:2).
2. Make disciples (Matt. 28:19–20).
3. Glorify God with their bodies (1 Cor. 6:19–20).
4. Seek to live in unity with fellow believers (John 17:21).
5. Serve others using their gifts (1 Pet. 4:9–10).
6. Trust the Lord to direct their steps (Prov. 16:9).
7. Be compassionate and humble (1 Pet. 3:8–9).
8. Live at peace with everyone (Rom. 12:18).
9. Use their words to build others up (Eph. 4:29).
10. Know the voice of their Shepherd and not be led astray (John 10:4–5).
11. Feed on the Word of God and grow into spiritual maturity (Heb. 5:11–14).
12. Don't drift away (Heb. 2:1).
13. Be known for their faith in Christ (Col. 1:3–4).
14. Be committed to growing in godliness (1 Tim. 4:7).
15. Tell future generations about the Lord (Ps. 78:1–8).
16. Joyfully submit to church leaders in authority (Heb. 13:17).
17. Have a teachable attitude (Prov. 4:1).
18. Be slow to anger (James 1:19).
19. Forgive one another (Eph. 4:32).
20. Bear fruit and grow in the knowledge of God (Col. 1:10).
21. Live according to the Spirit (Rom. 8:4).

THREE

Assembling and Leading a Strong Ministry Team

> He makes the whole body fit together perfectly. As each part does its own special work, it helps the other parts grow, so that the whole body is healthy and growing and full of love.
>
> Ephesians 4:16 NLT

I understand the temptation you might have to do it all yourself. It's so much simpler for us to just do things the way we want to do them, but it's not God's best. It's nearly impossible for just one person to plan and execute every activity and event. At some point, even the most organized, driven woman will find she needs to ask for help, if she doesn't burn out or bail first. As you'll see in this chapter, the benefits of utilizing a team or teams of women are numerous and biblical. While the instructions and tips that follow won't guarantee love and unity at all times, there's a peace that follows when you know for certain that you've prayerfully asked women to serve in the areas they are gifted in.

Wisdom from the Word

What does God's Word say about leaders and teamwork? In the Old Testament, Moses is called by God to care for His people, the Israelites. In

Exodus 18, Jethro, Moses's father-in-law, notices the task before Moses is much too great for one man to do alone. Jethro tells him, "What you are doing is not good. You and these people who come to you will only wear yourselves out. The work is too heavy for you; you cannot handle it alone" (vv. 17–18). Jethro instructs Moses to recruit others to share his load and make it lighter (v. 22). Moses listened to his father-in-law and chose capable men to lead groups of people.

Paul is an example in the New Testament of a leader who valued teamwork. Paul regularly traveled with others who helped to share the gospel and encourage the people in the churches they visited. For example, Barnabas traveled with Paul on his first missionary journey (Acts 13). His involvement increased Paul's influence and effectiveness.

> The name Barnabas means "son of encouragement," and encouragement was his first function in Paul's life. When the newly converted Saul/Paul came to the Christians at Jerusalem, they were afraid of him. But Barnabas built a bridge between Saul and the other Christians, vouching for the reality of his faith and ministry.[1]

Jesus also understood the value of leaders working in teams. He had a team of twelve disciples who spent approximately three years learning from Him in preparation for what was to come. In Mark 6:7, Jesus called together those twelve disciples and sent them out two by two to call people to repentance.

God's Word is clear that we are not supposed to do ministry alone. Every member of the team is important and has a God-given gift to use to bless others. Just as Barnabas's gift was encouragement, the women in your church have gifts that can expand the impact of your women's ministry program. Paul uses the picture of a physical body to help us understand the importance of the church body working together for God's glory: "He makes the whole body fit together perfectly. As each part does its own special work, it helps the other parts grow, so that the whole body is healthy and growing and full of love" (Eph. 4:16 NLT). You and I are just one part of the body. It's God's design that we invite other women to serve alongside us. We need other women to do their part so our church body and our ministry are healthy, growing, and full of love!

Ministry Memory

I'm still not sure why Kara blew through our entire food budget at one meeting. Upon hearing the surprise and panic in my voice when I asked how much she'd spent, one of the wiser, older women on our team graciously covered the expense out of her own pocket, saving me from explaining this oversight to the church staff. While that may have kept me from begging for additional budget money, it didn't stop the voice in my head that demanded to know what Kara had been thinking.

When Kara joined our team midyear, I had some concerns. Because of her friendship with many of the women on our team, there had been no discussion about whether she was the right person for this position. Despite my role as co-leader, I wasn't asked for my input but was told she would be joining the team. I wish I could report that was the one and only time our team failed to work together, but it was just one example of a tumultuous year. That year, I learned the very costly lesson of what happens when you fail to build a team God's way.

How to Build a Team

Assembling a team should always start with dedicated time in prayer. Round up a few prayer warriors to meet regularly to pray for the formation of your women's ministry team. As you pray, ask God to reveal who needs to be on the team. Ask Him to prepare the hearts of the women He wants for the task. As God brings to mind different women in your church, confirm with the other members of your prayer team that each name should be on the list you're building. Don't ask anyone yet, though. There are a few more steps you'll want to take that I'll outline below.

It may be tempting to transition a prayer team (if you have one) into the initial women's ministry team. However, please don't assume that your prayer warriors are also supposed to serve on the ministry team. Some may feel called. Some may not. Make each woman's name a matter of prayer.

Don't forget to look beyond your circle of friends and acquaintances at church. Your women benefit when the team includes women of different ages, different social circles, and different seasons of life. They'll help you remember women whose experiences differ from your own. (I've got some tips to help you find them, don't worry!)

How Big of a Team Do You Need?

That very first women's ministry team I assembled started with just three of us. That was it. For a church with about seven hundred members, it felt like a tiny team, but it was what God gave us, so we trusted Him. Slowly, He added to our numbers, and we created separate teams for retreat and conference planning. It worked, even when it seemed like it wouldn't.

I'm sure you're wondering, *What's a good size for my team?* A seasoned leader I know recommends one team member for every one hundred women in your church. However, my teams have often been smaller or larger than that size. I do think it's possible to have a team that's too big. If you oversee a large women's ministry, you may want to max out at twelve, with those leaders overseeing sub-teams. Make it a matter of prayer, and trust God's timing and provision for your specific situation.

If you're hesitant, please know I understand. I'm a recovering prefer-to-do-it-myself-er. Teams of women can be a lot of work between delegating, following up, and handling the challenges that can occur along the way. Even if it seems like the benefits of solo leading far outweigh the cons, what God has to say overrules any hesitation or preferences we might have.

In addition to Paul using the metaphor of the body to help the Ephesian church understand the importance of working together, he also writes in Romans:

> For by the grace given me I say to every one of you: Do not think of yourself more highly than you ought, but rather think of yourself with sober judgment, in accordance with the faith God has distributed to each of you. For just as each of us has one body with many members, and these members do not all have the same function, so in Christ we, though many, form one body, and each member belongs to all the others. We have different gifts, according to the grace given to each of us. If your gift is prophesying, then prophesy in accordance with your faith; if it is serving, then serve; if it is teaching, then teach; if it is to encourage, then give encouragement; if it is

> giving, then give generously; if it is to lead, do it diligently; if it is to show mercy, do it cheerfully. (12:3–8)

The church body, working together and utilizing their gifts, helps the church to flourish and grow. God's Word makes it clear that when we invite other women to use the unique gifts He has given them, God is glorified and our ministry is better for it.

Roles and Responsibilities

Do you need to divide the work of women's ministry among the members of your team? Should the same person be responsible for publicity, food, or decorations at each event? If you're seeking to follow the examples in God's Word, I would argue yes. While not every team I've served on has formally divided responsibilities, those that did ran more smoothly. On my current team, Jenna is great with games, Ann has a gift for decorating, Samantha does a fabulous job organizing the food and prepping the coffee, and I help with publicity and often teach. While I could find an idea for our table decor online, it's not something that comes easy or natural for me. It's not one of my gifts, but it is Ann's gift. Constantly swapping roles and responsibilities can lead to confusion, overlap, and even conflict. Placing team members in roles that align with their gifts fosters harmony and purpose.

Practically speaking, when we ask women to serve in a specific role with specific responsibilities:

- The hard work of hosting an event is shared among the members of the team.
- Team members refine and improve their tasks as they learn and adjust from one event to another, decreasing the chances that missteps or mistakes will be repeated.
- Unity among team members grows as they support each other's efforts.
- Team members flourish as they serve in their area of gifting.
- Division of tasks is understood and respected.

Team leaders who fail to define roles and responsibilities can hinder the success of their team.

There are many ways to structure your team. Your church bylaws may determine your team structure. If you are unsure, or your church does not have bylaws, consult your pastor and ask for advice. Regardless, you'll need a women's ministry leader (or co-leader, with duties divided) for your team. (Some churches use the term "women's ministry director" or "women's ministry coordinator.") It's hard to make progress forward if there isn't a clear team lead. Practically, your church staff needs a point person to communicate with, and the women in your church need to know who to contact about women's ministry events and activities.

Five Recommended Women's Ministry Team Roles

Generally speaking, it can be helpful to have at least these five roles on your women's ministry team:

1. Women's ministry director: communicates with the church staff, sets the agenda, and casts the vision.
2. Publicity coordinator: creates and distributes publicity. Coordinates social media accounts.
3. Bible study (discipleship) coordinator: oversees selection of Bible studies, creates the schedule, and trains group leaders.
4. Hospitality coordinator: manages greeters, food, and decorations.
5. Event coordinator: coordinates planning for larger events such as retreats, conferences, and banquets.

Additional Team Roles

Depending upon the size of your church and focus of your women's ministry program, you may want to divide some of the roles listed above or expand beyond them. Here are some additional roles your team may deem essential:

- Prayer coordinator: provides prayer support for events and trains prayer team members who will pray with attendees at some events.

- Retreat coordinator: organizes and leads retreat plans.
- Treasurer: tracks ministry expenses and reimburses team members.
- Food coordinator: manages the food selections, researches caterers, and coordinates food sign-ups as needed for each event.
- Decorations coordinator: oversees all decorations for the event, including color selections and table decorations.
- Registration coordinator: creates online registration forms and plans for any in-person registration needs.
- Encouragement coordinator: might oversee a notecard ministry or blessing baskets for specific needs such as hospital stays, grief, or newborns.
- Secretary: takes meeting minutes and distributes them after each meeting.
- Music or worship coordinator: oversees song selections and selects singers and musicians.
- Childcare coordinator: secures appropriate childcare staffing and plans activities for each age group.

Additionally, if you have season-specific women's groups (widows, moms, single women, divorced moms, empty nesters, homeschooling moms, and so on), you may want leaders from each group to be part of your team so you can support them and they can share what's happening with the women they serve.

Meeting Your Unique Needs

What works in one church might not work in another. Prioritize and pray. Give God license to create a team that aligns with your women's ministry mission statement, if you have one (we'll discuss that soon), and your church's mission statement. You may not need a treasurer, discipleship leader, or childcare coordinator if other church staff members, deacons, or elders will assist in those areas. You'll also need to consider other ministries in your church. If you have a missions ministry, do they plan women's mission events, or would it be helpful to have someone on your women's ministry team in that role? It may be better to partner with other ministry teams in your church than to duplicate their efforts.

Last, if you already have a team in place but no roles or responsibilities assigned, decide as a team what roles are needed. Consider asking each team member to take a spiritual gifts test (search "spiritual gifts assessment" or "spiritual gifts survey," if there isn't one your church prefers you use). You may wish to meet one-on-one with each team member to pray about and discuss which role would allow them to best serve according to their gifts. If more than one woman feels called to a role, co-leaders may be the best option. It is possible that some of your women may step down, in which case you can work through the process of adding new team members—this time with a specific role in mind.

How to Ask Women to Serve on Your Team

Now that we've established that teams are godly, good, and necessary, and we've determined which roles to fill, let's work through how to fill each role with the right person. As I mentioned at the beginning of this chapter, it's important to have a process in place for adding new team members. The team I mentioned in this chapter's Ministry Memory did not have a process for inviting women to serve with us, and I'm embarrassed to admit we didn't even pray about it. I know that critical misstep led to most of our troubles, as it was a difficult and hard year with very little unity. God allowed us to reap the consequences of our disobedience.

That second year, though, God redeemed our ministry through a difficult breakup of our team and by way of Julie, the new adviser for our group. Julie taught me how to prayerfully build a new team. The difference between our two teams was startling! God led us to ask women who weren't even on my radar but were perfect for the task. There was a sweetness, a unity, and a spirit of prayer that permeated everything we did.

Since then, I've replicated this five-step process with great success. It will work whether you are recruiting new team members or adding to an established women's ministry team. You'll make a list, ask them to serve, guide them to seek wisdom, pray for them, and then wait for their answer.

Step 1: Make a List

Start by putting together a list of names. Pray God will put women in your path. Expect Him to bring them to you. Keep your eyes open—they may not be who you expect. Write each name down. Ask for suggestions from wise, godly people like your pastors, pastors' spouses, and trusted small group leaders. Use suggestions from your women's ministry team if you have one. As you ask for names, be specific. Explain what position you are looking to fill, what the role involves, and what kind of person you are looking for. For example, "We are looking for someone warm, outgoing, and friendly to serve as our hospitality team leader."

When you've got your list of potential team members, submit the name(s) to the pastoral staff for approval. Your church may have certain requirements for serving in leadership roles, such as church membership, active attendance, and personal recommendations. Make sure you abide by those requirements. There's no sense in asking the team to pray over a name if that person isn't qualified to lead at this time.

Finally, take your list and pray over it. You and your team need to spend time in prayer over the person and the position. Ask the Holy Spirit to give each team member discernment. As hard as this sounds, ask God to confirm names on your list or even remove them. If there isn't unity, set that name aside for now.

Step 2: Ask Them to Serve

When the pastoral staff and your team agree on a name, then it's time for the next step: Ask them to join the team! This is not the time to send a quick text or to grab them in the hallway between services and pop the question. Instead, try to find a time to meet over coffee or call them on the phone. When we take the time to be *intentional* in the way in which we ask someone to serve, it communicates the weight of the ask and the need for prayerful consideration on their part.

Here are a few tips on how to ask someone to join your women's ministry team. First, introduce yourself. Share a little bit about your role on the team. If you've got a connection, such as your boys are in the same Sunday school class, be sure to mention it. Next, explain why you are calling/meeting. Let them know there is an opening on the women's ministry leadership team for [insert position] and that their name was suggested. (One important note: I never reveal my source, as it can add unwanted pressure to say yes, and that source may not share names with me ever again.) If possible, share why they would be a good fit. For example, "Susie, you always make everyone feel welcome. God's given you a heart and a gift for hospitality."

Ask them to pray about it and ask them to call you back by a specific date. Julie advised me to give them one week to pray about the decision. A few years later, another mentor encouraged me to narrow the response window down to just seventy-two hours. When I shared that I always gave women one week, she challenged me, "Don't you think God could give them an answer in three days?" I've since adjusted my approach and usually follow up in three days' time. Waiting a whole week for a yes or no can drag out the process, especially if you receive multiple rejections.

Step 3: Guide Them to Seek Wisdom

Many of your women may need some additional guidance in knowing if God's calling them to join your team or not. Encourage them to discern the Lord's will through prayer and Scripture. I often share a recent personal example of how I sought and followed the Holy Spirit's leading. Additionally, they may find it helpful to seek godly guidance from a trusted mentor.

If you are married or have a family, you may understand how women's ministry events, especially those in the evening and on weekends, can impact the family schedule. You may miss a baseball game or two. If you're away for a weekend retreat, other family members may be impacted by your absence. Please encourage them to talk with their spouse, if applicable, about this decision and the time commitment it requires.

Ask if they have any questions and answer them as honestly as you can. If they don't ask about what the position involves or team expectations (such as meeting monthly), share those with them. You don't have to get overly detailed at this point—just give them a general overview. You don't want to scare them off, but you also want them to understand the level of commitment that is expected.

Step 4: Pray for Them

Now that you've guided them to discern the Lord's will, talk about the position with their spouse, and answered any questions they have, it's time to pray. End your time together by praying for them. Yes, out loud, in person or over the phone with them. You may feel led to pray for wisdom, for their conversation with their spouse, or for discernment to know if this is where God wants them to serve next. After you've prayed for them, wrap it up. Thank them for their time and remind them you look forward to hearing from them by the date you've given.

Step 5: Wait for Their Answer

Now it's time to wait. As you wait, continue to pray for their response to be in line with God's will. If you cross paths during the time you've given them to pray, try not to rush their decision. Trust God is working while you wait. If they do not call you back by the designated day (and many will not), call them the very next day. If they ask for an extension, graciously give them one more day. If God hasn't given them a clear yes by then, it's okay to assume His answer is no or not right now. If He wants them to be part of the team, He will do it some other way or some other time.

Tips:

- Try not to take an answer, either yes or no, during that first meeting. You want them to seek God's will and speak with their spouse, if applicable. However, if they are adamantly against serving, end the conversation graciously and thank them for their time.
- If they say they are too busy, be understanding and sympathetic. If you can, kindly remind them that God can expand our time or may lead us to take something else off our plate to make room for something new. Encourage them to pray and seek God's will.
- Graciously accept the answer you receive. It can be really hard to hear a no when you are confident God is calling them to serve. You've been obedient to ask.

I'll admit I used to dread these conversations until God helped me to see what great opportunities they are. Even the no answers have given me the chance to get to know some of our women better and have provided some great teaching moments about seeking God's will. They do get easier over time, and the benefits far outweigh the discomfort.

Please notice I did not suggest posting a "help wanted" ad. You're recruiting women for a leadership position, and, as such, there should be a vetting process. If you advertise an open leadership position, you limit yourself to those who apply, and if only one person responds, you're stuck with them. Just because someone is willing to serve doesn't mean they are called to serve.

You're recruiting women for a leadership position, and, as such, there should be a vetting process.

Remember, your team should reflect the makeup of your church and include women of different ages, stages, and social circles. If you find you're struggling to reach a specific age group at your women's ministry meetings, pray for a way to add a member of that group to your team. For example, many leaders struggle to reach younger women but have not asked a younger woman to serve on their team. More diverse insights and experiences can help us be more effective. A multigenerational team is more likely to develop into a multigenerational ministry. Many leaders also find that including past team leaders and pastors' wives as advisers to their team is of great value. Their experience can provide invaluable insight and direction.

Sometimes we assume the senior pastor's wife will take on the role of women's ministry leader. This form of nepotism can be problematic for the church. Not only may she not be the best woman for the job, but she might also not want the job! To my knowledge, no other ministry in the church operates this way, nor should it. Our intent should be to prayerfully recruit women to whom God has given a gift and passion for women's ministry.

The process of building a team could take a few weeks, a couple of months, or be ongoing. God likely won't fill every role immediately. He may never fill them all! Get started and trust He'll add women to your team in His perfect timing. We're walking in obedience, not waiting for perfection.

How Long Should Women Serve?

If your church has bylaws with term limits for committees/teams, you'll need to abide by those guidelines. If not, this is something you'll want to discuss and determine before you find yourself trying to remove a leader who needs to step down. Term limits can provide some protection, but there are pros and cons.

Term limits can:

- Prevent leadership burnout.
- Protect the ministry from long-term damage if the leader isn't successful.
- Provide the opportunity for other women to lead.
- Bring much-needed change, fresh energy, and new ideas to a stale ministry.
- Remove leaders who would otherwise remain in place to the detriment of the ministry.
- Attract women who may be unwilling to serve in a never-ending role.

However, term limits can also:

- Create a lack of continuity, as each new leader casts a unique vision.
- Prevent some initiatives from taking root because every leader has her own thing she would like to do.
- Require reestablishing relationships that have been developed within your community.
- Force great leaders out of the role.
- Cause the position to sit empty if a new leader cannot be found quickly, compelling women's ministry events and activities to discontinue in the interim.
- Risk us overstepping our bounds by removing someone whom God has not called out of service.

Whether or not you or your church implements term limits, you'll need to create a process for knowledge transfer and training new leaders. It's also imperative that church leadership reviews the effectiveness of women's ministry team leaders and has a process in place for replacing leaders when necessary. Those serving also need to be provided a way to exit graciously when they sense God moving them into a different ministry. Many teams have found that asking leaders to recommit every one or two years helps to smooth that process. Staggering the start of terms can also increase the team's success by balancing the team with seasoned and new members.

Team Meetings

Regularly scheduled in-person team meetings are essential—not just for planning but also for prayer and for building community and unity among members. Once you have at least one team member, you'll need to decide when, where, and how often to meet.

Scheduling

While it may be tempting to only meet as needed (everyone is busy), my advice is to meet monthly. If possible, find a regular day and time each month (for example, every third Monday at 6:30 p.m.).

Meeting monthly:

- Allows your team to touch base at regular intervals.
- Provides an opportunity to address old and new business.
- Offers consistency, especially when meeting the same day, time, and place.
- Keeps the team connected, which is especially beneficial in a larger church or one with multiple services.
- Bathes your ministry regularly in prayer.

When will you meet and for how long? Daytime meetings can be convenient if your team members are available. However, only meeting in the daytime could keep women with inflexible work schedules or those who have childcare needs from being able to serve on the team. As for your meeting length, I suggest one and a half to two hours.

Agenda

Now that we covered the logistics, let's move on to the content. Having sat in meetings with and without agendas, I believe agendas directly affect the success of our meetings. Every team meeting should have one. In most cases, the women's ministry team leader or co-leader will create the agenda, with input as needed from other team members.

Agendas can:

- Give your team time to prepare and pray over agenda items when they are distributed before the meeting. No one likes to be surprised. Give God time to speak to their hearts.
- Ensure a level of accountability—both for you and for the team. If it's written down, it's more likely to happen.
- Keep the discussion on track and focused. I've often pointed to my agenda and reminded the team, "We have a lot to cover; we need to keep moving."

When coupled with meeting minutes, agendas provide a reference for decisions and action items. Email a copy of the minutes to all team members no later than a week after you've met. You may also wish to keep a copy of the minutes in a physical binder or a digital folder to reference when a question comes up during your meetings.

Agendas model organization. When you are organized and prepared, it encourages and models that behavior for your team. While it may not come naturally to all of us, we can all learn to organize our meetings and thoughts. Agendas also remind team members of their responsibilities. If team members are expected to share an update, project, idea, or similar, noting that on the agenda serves as a gentle reminder. I like to place the names of our team members behind the agenda items for which they are responsible.

If possible, send out your agenda one week before the team meeting. Use that email to remind your team of the meeting location and time. Be sure to include any other related notes, lists, and spreadsheets they will need. Sending out the agenda in advance allows women to contact you before the meeting if they have concerns or information to share. Such pre-meeting discussions can add necessary clarity and avoid possible confrontations or division.

Content

There is much you could and should cover when your team meets together. The women's ministry leader or co-leader should take charge and run your team meeting, moving along the conversation as needed and reining in the conversation if it gets off track.

1. You may wish to begin each meeting with an icebreaker game to build unity and develop relationships among team members. The better your women know each other, the better they'll be able to communicate with each other and extend grace to one another.
2. Before digging in to your meeting agenda, be sure to pray! Don't ask only for a blessing on your plans but also ask God what He wants your team to do. Ask Him to direct and order your steps. Pray also for the women in your church and community. If your agenda is light, you may have time to pray for your women by name if you are in a small church. Many leaders like to provide each team member with an opportunity to share praises and prayer requests with the rest of the team. You may want to set a limit of one or two personal and ministry-related requests to keep your meeting moving.
3. You may wish to follow your prayer time with a short testimony, teaching from the Word, or training.
4. Wrap up any old business left over from the previous meeting and then move into the upcoming events and activities. You can organize your agenda by event, team member, or a combination of both.

If team members are working on an upcoming event or activity, a progress update should be expected. If you empower your team members, you won't need to use the bulk of your meeting time for event planning. Big decisions such as event themes, speakers, dates, and times can be set by either the women's ministry director or the event team leader. Smaller decisions such as napkin color and program design can be delegated. If we want our leaders to grow, we must give them opportunities to lead. You'll find your agenda moves along much more quickly when leaders share a status report rather than debate decisions.

I find it helpful to decide in advance approximately how much time we'll need to discuss each item on the agenda. I only note the time for each item on my copy of the agenda, because I know God may move us along a bit faster or slow us down for a needed discussion along the way.

Creating a standard meeting agenda is another way to keep things running smoothly. Team members quickly learn what's expected. (You'll find a sample women's ministry team meeting agenda in the resources section at the end of this chapter.)

Crafting a Mission Statement

You may have heard that leading a women's ministry is like herding cats. It's funny, but there's truth in it—your team may get distracted by different ideas they find online or on social media. Defining the mission of your women's ministry as a team will help guide the ministry calendar and focus your efforts.

Here are three keys I've found to be helpful in crafting a ministry mission statement:

1. Your women's ministry mission statement should align closely with the mission of your church. You want to complement that mission, not compete against it. You may have heard people refer to women's ministry as a silo ministry. You are not a silo. You are one arm of the church body.
2. Your mission statement should be used as a plumb line from which to base future decisions. All activities, ideas, and events your ministry produces should fit within the boundaries of your mission statement.
3. Crafting or revising a mission statement should be a team project. This is so important. Please don't miss this. If you are the team leader, director, or whatever you call that position, God may have

> given you a vision for your ministry or for the year to share with your team—and that's great. But mission statements aren't just for the season that you're serving; they should last for years far beyond your service. Mission statements should also transition easily to new team members. And writing a mission statement as a team creates unity, as you're working together to craft a shared vision.

Spend time in prayer before your meeting and ask God to give you direction specifically about your mission statement.

You may find it helpful to remind your team of the five essential ingredients for women's ministry—prayer, care, theology, evangelism, and discipleship—as you write your mission statement. You might also want to guide your team through these questions to help them articulate what's most important:

- What is our goal?
- Who are we trying to reach?
- How are we going to reach them/how are we going to accomplish that goal?
- Does this encompass what we do and what we believe God wants us to do?
- Does this mission statement align with and complement our church's mission statement?
- Does it exalt Jesus Christ and glorify God?

(I've also included a mission statement worksheet in the resources section at the end of this chapter to help your team work through these questions.)

Here's one example of a women's ministry mission statement:

> The women's ministry team at Christ Community exists to build up the church, disciple women, and evangelize the lost by offering events and activities that are biblically focused and address the spiritual needs of women, providing opportunities for service, and promoting fellowship for our church and community, thereby encouraging and strengthening each woman's relationship with Jesus Christ.

Take the time between meetings to pray and meditate on your mission statement before finalizing it, allowing the Holy Spirit to make known any areas that need clarity or editing. Also be sure to share it with the pastor who oversees your women's ministry team and get their stamp of approval as well before you publish it anywhere.

Once you have a mission statement, what do you do with it? First, make it as visible as possible. Put it on your website, on your social media pages and groups, and in your event programs. Share it regularly with the women in your church. It should become familiar to them. They might even memorize it if it's short enough. As your team makes plans, make sure each idea supports your mission statement. If it doesn't, ask women how it could. It's easier to give a yes or no answer to ideas when you have a mission statement to point back to.

The information we've gone over in this chapter is so very important in building a team that functions well, and it is tempting to stop here. However, there are two more nonessentials that will so greatly benefit your women's ministry team I can't leave them out. Please don't see them as more things to do but rather as tools that will help your team function at its best—with each part of the body operating optimally.

Team Planning Meetings and Retreats

Team planning meetings are something I wish I'd implemented early on. The team I currently serve on takes an annual planning retreat. In years past, we've headed down to the beach for one night. The mix of fellowship and planning has helped our team bond and create some great memories. We still laugh about the time one of our vehicles almost ran out of gas on the way home! Typically, during this retreat we review our plan for the rest of the year and brainstorm the calendar for the next year. We're able to discuss new projects and program ideas that don't normally fit into our monthly meeting agenda.

You may find it helpful to include time for your team to reflect on what's working well and what changes they'd like to see. Consider sharing these three questions with your team a few days prior to your planning meeting so they can process, ponder, and pray:

- What do you think God is asking our women's ministry to start doing that we are not doing?
- What do you sense God is bringing to an end or asking us to stop doing?
- What is our women's ministry doing that you believe God wants us to continue doing?

I admit, when I first began leading in women's ministry, I hesitated to ask my team members to give up any more time out of their busy schedules. I knew a concentrated time of planning would benefit the team and our women, yet it seemed like too big of an ask. Now that I serve on a team that has an annual team retreat, I thank God our director sees the need. Our women's ministry calendar flows much better, and mapping out our year in advance has removed that pressure of "What do we do next?"

Team Covenant

I can't tell you how many leaders have reached out asking for advice on dealing with team members who aren't showing up at meetings or following through on their commitments. Some offer flimsy excuses, while others don't seem to understand the importance of following through. Crafting a team covenant, while not essential, can help set firm expectations and provide a framework for course corrections. If problems arise, you'll be able to refer to the commitment your team member has made.

One team I served on in the past was particularly challenging. While we all had a passion for women's ministry, we often disagreed on what we should offer and how ideas should be implemented. Looking back now, it's obvious there was a lack of unity, love, and grace for one another. Meetings often became heated as the stronger personalities would battle it out while others shrank back and fell silent. More than I care to admit, I fell into the first group. I often returned home from our team meetings frustrated and near tears. Serving on a women's ministry team shouldn't have been that hard. I'd been a part of teams that worked well before; what were we missing?

Imagine my surprise when our director flipped the page to reveal a team covenant during one of our meetings. She knew it was time to set some expectations so we could move forward and function as a team. Viewing those expectations in writing and then signing our names in agreement was what our team needed to get back on track.

Don't wait until your team begins to fracture to put some expectations on behavior and attitudes in place. Team covenants can be a great preventive for un-Christlike behavior. Like your mission statement, you may wish to make this a group project. (A sample team covenant can be found in the resources section at the end of this chapter.)

Reflection Questions

1. What, if any, changes to your team structure does your team need to prayerfully consider?

2. If your team has a mission statement, please write it below. If not, what are some things you would like to see included in a mission statement?

3. List at least one tip you plan to implement when asking a woman to serve in a leadership role.

4. Do you have term limits? Explain why you think they are or are not needed in your church.

5. What did you find most encouraging or challenging in this chapter?

Praying Through the Process

Lord, You have given the women in our church many gifts. Please help us to identify and encourage the use of these gifts. When our team gathers to meet, please guide our decisions and our conversations so You are glorified. Where our team is lacking, whether that be in number or in unity, we ask You to supply what is needed so we can serve the women in our church well. Amen.

Sample Women's Ministry Team Meeting Agenda

- Icebreaker game or question
- Group prayer
- Teaching, testimony, or training
- Old business
- New business (listed out by topic or by position)
- Action items (highlight who, what, and when)
- Prayer

Sample Team Covenant

As a member of the women's ministry team:

I will work to fulfill the duties for my role and complete my responsibilities to the best of my ability. If I find I am ever unable to do so, I will immediately notify the team director.

I commit to pray for the other women on the team and will build them up with genuine words of encouragement and offer help when appropriate.

I will be open to spiritual conversations and learn to share my faith story with others.

I will prioritize my life, being a good steward of my time so that women's ministry does not become a burden.

I will be "outreach oriented." I will reach out to others during women's ministry events and activities, and I will do my best to recognize the needs of women in our group and meet them when appropriate.

I will strive to be a good role model, not behaving in ways that would cause another person to stumble.

____

Name

____

Date

Mission Statement Worksheet

1. What is our goal?

2. Who are we trying to reach?

3. How are we going to reach them/how are we going to accomplish that goal?

4. Write out the rough draft of the mission statement below:

5. Does this encompass what we do and what we believe God wants us to do?

6. Does this mission statement align with and complement our church's mission statement?

7. Does it exalt Jesus and glorify God?

FOUR

Discipleship Pathways

Bible Study, Mentoring, and More

> All Scripture is God-breathed and is useful for teaching, rebuking, correcting and training in righteousness, so that the servant of God may be thoroughly equipped for every good work.
>
> 2 Tim. 3:16–17

If we want women to taste and see that the Lord is good (Ps. 34:8), we must encourage them to feast on God's Word. You may recall discipleship was one of the five essential ingredients of a solid women's ministry program, and for good reason! God's Word is where we find salvation. God uses His Word for sanctification, making us more like Christ. Women who know the Word will desire to live out the Word.

In this chapter, we'll examine some of the different ways your women's ministry program might invite women to regularly engage with God's Word and discuss it with others. My goal is not to change the way you're implementing Bible study or discipleship but to encourage you to assess if what you're offering meets the needs of your women and supports the goals of your church and to consider changes that would strengthen what you provide. I understand the challenges of selecting biblically sound materials that encourage women to study what the Bible says. I'll introduce you to the READ Bible study format, and I'll share tips for selecting and vetting Bible studies.

Wisdom from the Word

What does God's Word say about itself? That seems like a strange question to ask, but the Bible has a lot to say about how we should think about the words in its sixty-six books. The Bible is unique. In 2 Timothy 3:16, Paul tells us "all Scripture is God-breathed." What does that mean? As 2 Peter 1:21 explains, "prophets . . . spoke from God as they were carried along by the Holy Spirit." We can trust God's Word because it is inspired by the Holy Spirit, who led its writers to pen the words we hold in our hands today.

As we continue reading 2 Timothy 3:16–17, we see why Scripture is useful. Paul says, "All Scripture is God-breathed and is useful for teaching, rebuking, correcting and training in righteousness, so that the servant of God may be thoroughly equipped for every good work." I love the way Warren Wiersbe breaks down this passage: God's Word helps us to know what is right (teaching), what is not right (rebuking), how to get right (correcting), and how to stay right (training in righteousness).[1] Pointing women to God's Word at every opportunity will help them know what is right, what's not right, how to get right, and how to stay right. Paul knows that the Word of God will help Timothy hold fast in the midst of persecution, suffering, and false teaching. It can do the same for us today too.

God's Word describes itself using words we might not expect. David describes it as worth more than gold and sweeter than honey in Psalm 19:10. God's Word is something we should desire and find enjoyable. Earlier, in verse 7, David says, "The law of the Lord is perfect, reviving the soul" (ESV). We should view God's Word as perfect and life-giving. Verse 8 reads, "the precepts of the Lord are right, rejoicing the heart" (ESV). We can trust that God's Word is right, and it should bring us joy.

God's Word is more than useful; it is necessary for living a godly life. Seeing all that Scripture is and does, we should prioritize the study of God's Word in our women's ministry program.

Ministry Memory

I'll be forever amazed at the way God puts women together to study the Bible. As I prayed and pondered over what to share in this chapter, the Lord brought two precious women from one group to mind. These women were the youngest and oldest members, respectively, of our Bible study group.

Maylee was a young mom with two boys under the age of three. The younger often sat on her hip or in her lap as she shared what she had learned that week. Despite caring for and chasing after two little boys, Maylee was dedicated to our Bible study group. She was determined to complete the homework and attend each week. Sometimes a sick child would keep her away, but we always looked forward to hearing how the Holy Spirit had spoken to her through God's Word. Maylee had a beautiful story of international adoption and an amazing story of how she came to know Christ that she eventually shared with us. Experiencing God's Word through her eyes brought fresh excitement to our study.

Barbara was the senior saint of our group that year. She was the most stylish and wisest of us all. She loved Jesus and always gave Him the credit. When Barbara answered a Bible study question, we all sat in rapt attention to hear what the Lord had imparted to her. Her quick wit and quips would leave us in stitches. Barbara had a story for everything, and each one glorified the Lord. She loved others well and was a great inspiration to all of us.

It's been many years since I sat in that Bible study group, yet I have not forgotten Barbara or Maylee. I'm thankful I'm still connected to Maylee through social media and get a glimpse every now and then of her growing family. They've since moved to another state, and God is now using *her* to pour into the young women at their church. Someday I hope to be someone's Barbara, sharing colorful stories of the great things I've seen God do.

Shifting Terms

What does Bible study look like in your church? As churches seek to better meet the needs of their members, they often rebrand or tweak current ministry practices. This has certainly been the case as it relates to Bible study. There's been a shift over time away from "Sunday school" to "small groups" and from "Bible study" to "discipleship groups" as pastors have sought to connect more men and women to each other and God's Word. By the time you read this, it's possible the pendulum has swung back or new terms have replaced these.

Your church's specific discipleship plan will factor heavily into what you offer. Remember, we always want to complement and not compete with other opportunities women have to study God's Word in community with others. Bible studies have experienced some subtle shifting in recent years. Daytime Bible studies have expanded to evening Bible study offerings, and many churches have added or changed to a discipleship group model. Here's where the verbiage can get confusing. Not every church, or even every ministry within the church, defines *discipleship* in the same way. What I view as discipleship, you may call small groups or something else. I'll define what the terms mean to me, and you are welcome to cross out any of my verbiage and replace it to align with your church's vernacular.

It all boils down to the emphasis on knowledge or relationships. Generally speaking, Bible studies and discipleship groups are focused more on knowledge, while small groups and mentoring are focused more on relationships. It's not that any exclude the other, but typically more time is dedicated to one over the other.

Bible study is typically a group of women (anywhere from five to fifteen, though sometimes more) who meet regularly (usually weekly) for a set period of time to go through a book of the Bible or a Bible study book together. There may be a time of teaching (led by someone in the church or via a teaching video) and a discussion time. Often there is homework to be done between meetings, though sometimes there is not. In some churches, the same group of women transitions to a new study. In other churches, there are multiple options and women select a new study at the start of each new session.

In some churches, discipleship groups and Bible study groups are synonymous. In the church I currently attend, our discipleship groups are for those who want to go deeper into God's Word. They are smaller, same-sex groups of three to five people that meet weekly for a year and follow a Bible reading plan. Participants also complete a journal each week using the HEAR method (based on the teaching in *Replicate* by Robby Gallaty). There is a focus on accountability and making Christlike choices. Each group member also responds to accountability questions each week. The goal is replication (disciples making disciples). At the end of each year, groups are multiplied as some group members step out to launch new discipleship groups.

Our church also has small groups (some call them life groups or community groups) that meet weekly. Most are coed, and they discuss the week's sermon using a discussion guide. In some churches, small groups choose a book to read and discuss. These small groups are also focused on providing regular fellowship and service opportunities. Our small groups meet in the fall with a Christmas break and then in the winter and spring. We only offer traditional "Bible studies" during part of our winter (three-week) and summer (six-week) breaks from small groups. Our church leadership believes strongly in offering a variety of opportunities for people to study God's Word and to be in community with one another.

The chart below helps to communicate the emphasis of each practice. It's not to say you can't experience close relationships or have deep theological discussions in your small group, it's just that discipleship groups of three to five people studying a specific section of Scripture are more likely to go deep relationally and theologically.

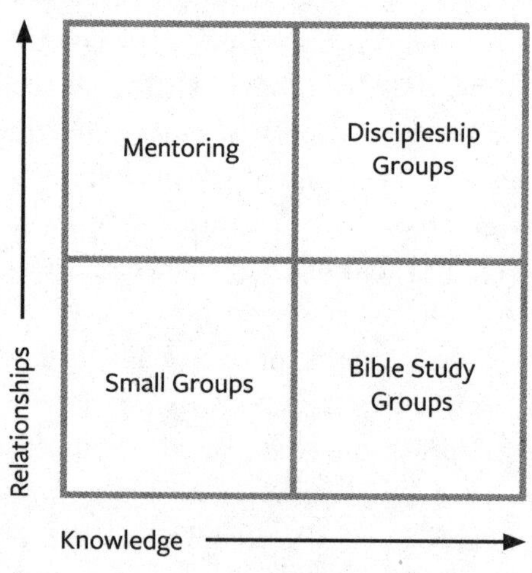

When you look at all the different opportunities your church offers for women to engage with God's Word, it may appear that all of them must be regularly reading and studying God's Word. *How could they not?* Several years ago, when I was at a previous church, my team put together a Bible Study Habit Survey. We wanted to capture a realistic view of the Bible study habits of the women in our church. I'll be honest, I assumed our women's personal Bible study habits were pretty decent until we administered the survey. My heart sank as I flipped through the cards they had filled out anonymously. Did our women really feel they had a preschool or elementary understanding of God's Word? Did they really find it boring? Outside of Sunday mornings, our women were not spending much time in God's Word at all. We may have suspected that was true, but we didn't want it to be. It was clear to our team that this was an area we needed to focus on. (You'll find this Bible study habits survey plus a Bible study health assessment in the resources section at the end of this chapter.) I pray, as you read through this section, the Holy Spirit will reveal any changes you may need to make so your women will truly delight in studying God's Word.

The READ Bible Study Method

In the summer of 2016, as I wrapped up another Bible study book session, the Lord began to convict me of the time I had spent in the Bible study book versus the time I had spent reading His Word. There was a big discrepancy. I was humbled and embarrassed at how little time I had spent in my Bible while in "Bible study." All summer long, I wrestled with the Lord over what needed to change. I didn't have a seminary degree, so how was I supposed to study the Bible on my own without a book, pastor, or author guiding me? I dove into books on how to study the Bible. Almost every resource recommended an inductive-style Bible study format founded upon the AIO method (application, interpretation, and observation). There was no need to reinvent the wheel. AIO needed to be the foundation of what I sensed God calling me to do.

By the end of the summer, the READ Bible study method was born, and I presented the rough draft to our Bible study coordinator, Donna, over lunch. I walked her through the steps—Record, Explore, Apply, and

Do—and shared with her the rough drafts of weekly worksheets that would lead women through the Bible to dig deep into one chapter a week and serve as the basis for our group discussion time. Donna shared the team had been praying for almost two years for God's clear direction for an inductive-style Bible study class. She agreed to review the materials and adopt the READ format beginning that fall semester. That ministry year, our women dug deep and studied their way through four books of the Bible. They learned how to uncover the cultural and historical context of the text, follow cross references, and see the bigger picture of God's story. We watched God transform our women through the regular reading and studying of His Word!

I cannot overemphasize the importance of biblical literacy. According to the Center for Biblical Engagement, "the life of someone who engages Scripture four or more times a week looks radically different from the life of someone who does not. In fact, the lives of Christians who do not engage with the Bible most days of the week look no different from the lives of non-believers."[2] Brace yourself for these findings—they are startling! Their study revealed that those who engage with the Bible four or more times a week are 228 percent more likely to share their faith with others, 407 percent more likely to memorize Scripture, 59 percent less likely to view pornography, and 30 percent less likely to struggle with loneliness.[3] And those were just the highlights! Regular engagement with God's Word will change the lives of your women.

Women don't just need to be regular readers of the Bible; they need to know and understand what it says. That may seem obvious, but my social media feed far too often features Scripture that has been taken out of context and quotes that are biblically inaccurate. Our women need to know what the Bible says so they can spot inaccurate teachings, not just on social media but everywhere. Almost every book in the New Testament warns of false teachings and false teachers. One way we protect our women against these false teachings is by ensuring they know what God's Word says.

Women Want to Discuss God's Word

The READ Bible study technique answered an unspoken need in our Bible study groups—women were hungry for more discussion time. This wasn't a unique need. Women in Bible studies everywhere are worn out from lengthy Bible study videos and frustrated with short discussion sessions. As we examine our Bible study schedules, we need to be sure to include time for our women to engage with the lesson.

Discussion groups allow women to:

- Process what they've studied.
- Practice talking about God and the Bible.
- Learn from other women (Titus 2:3–5).
- Hold one another accountable.

When the teams I've served on have sent out a survey at the end of our Bible study sessions, women always comment in large numbers about how much they enjoyed and benefited from the discussion time. The connections that are made and the sweet sharing that occurs are priceless. I never fail to be amazed at how God uses that discussion time to teach us more about Himself and to help us encourage one another.

Selecting the Best Bible Study for Your Women

I'm willing to wager that your regular Bible study ladies have a favorite Bible study author. And while that isn't a bad thing, many of our women have become dependent on someone, often a specific female someone, to lead them through the Bible. It's time we stop unintentionally fueling the belief that our women are not capable of studying the Word without a well-known author at the helm.

A well-known Bible study author should not be a requirement for selecting a Bible study. As I've already mentioned, your women can and should learn how to study God's Word on their own. I also realize that there are many fabulous Bible study books women would label as "life-changing." So, how do we decide what to do?

We must blanket our Bible study selection with prayer, asking the Lord to direct us to the best study for our specific group of women. We also need to determine who will make the Bible study selection for our groups. The group facilitator, a pastor, a women's ministry team Bible study coordinator, a Bible study review team, an attendee vote, or a combination of these might select your study. Here's a quick look at the pros and cons of each one.

Facilitator Selection

Pros—The facilitator is likely to pick a study topic she is passionate about, and that passion will shine through in her teaching and facilitating.

Cons—Facilitators sometimes get in a rut, repeatedly choosing the same authors. The selection(s) may not be in alignment with the current focus for the women's ministry or the church.

Pastor or Discipleship Director Selection

Pros—The women's ministry team does not have to delegate the task. The pastor/discipleship director is often aware of newer studies. The studies they choose will likely align with the church's beliefs, mission, or current focus.

Cons—If this person is a man, he may not choose something that appeals to many women. The facilitator and women's ministry team may feel they had no say in the selection.

Women's Ministry Team Bible Study Coordinator Selection

Pros—This is her primary role, so she should be familiar with a variety of studies and should have her pulse on the interests of the women in the church and community. As part of the women's ministry team, her selections should support and encourage the current focus of the women's ministry and the church.

Cons—Her preferences for a specific study style or author may be weighed more heavily in the decision-making process, though not necessarily intentionally. A facilitator may wish to have input. She may lack the discernment needed to spot false teaching.

Bible Study Review Team Selection

Pros—A wide variety of women come together to review and give input. A member of the women's ministry team or the Bible study coordinator should chair and guide the team, keeping them on task and in alignment with current church and ministry goals. Multiple people complete reviews of the same study.

Cons—There is a time commitment, and multiple meetings will be necessary. The majority rules, which may not always be a good thing.

Attendees Vote on the Selection

Pros—Those who attend are given a voice in the choice(s). If the women's ministry team or Bible study coordinator is struggling to narrow down the options, this can be a fair way of deciding which study or studies to offer.

Cons—The voters may be unfamiliar with the content of each study. The final selection may not be in alignment with church and ministry goals. Not all votes may be bathed in prayer.

For this last method, one option is to have attendees vote on the topic, but not on the specific study materials, which allows the facilitator to make sure the study is one that aligns with God's Word and the church's beliefs.

No matter which method is used, there are some key questions you'll want to answer as you prayerfully review possible studies in light of Scripture.

First, the practical questions:

- Who will participate in this study?
- What is the biblical literacy level of the women who will attend?
- Is this a topic, book, or character of the Bible that interests the group?
- How long is your meeting time?
- How many weeks will you be meeting?
- How much homework do you wish to assign?
- Do you need/want specific questions for your discussion time?
- What is your budget?
- What type of study are you looking for? (Bible, video-driven, Bible study book, Bible study workbook, combination, or sermon-based)

While there's some wiggle room in the answers to these practical questions, the theological questions are deal-breakers:

- Is this study biblically sound?
- Does this study emphasize engagement with the Scriptures, or is it focused primarily on the author's personal stories and experiences?
- Does the study encourage women to read and apply the Word of God to their lives?
- Does this study align with the beliefs and teachings of our pastor and church?
- What is the author's training and background? Does it align with what our church teaches?

- Does the study encourage prayerfully seeking both understanding and knowledge through the teaching of the Holy Spirit?
- Does this study encourage women to search the Scriptures for answers, or are they primarily found within the pages of a book or workbook?

How we select our Bible studies matters. When we use popular vote to select a study, we very well may miss selecting the best study for our women. And if we limit our selections to only female authors, we can miss out on some wonderful studies written by men.

Bible Study Homework

I have not forgotten this lesson presented in my college education class: When we set the bar high, our students will rise to meet it, but when we set the bar low, our students won't work to rise above it. The same holds true for Bible study.

I've heard leaders say:

"Our women won't do homework."

"They only like studies with a DVD."

"We don't want to scare new or young Christians away."

I hear concern and even love behind these excuses, but that is exactly what they are—excuses. We assume we know what's best for our women, often at the expense of their spiritual growth.

Years ago, a dear friend of mine, Morgan, decided she wanted to join Jill and me for a very homework-intensive Bible study at our church. Morgan had never attended a Bible study before, and we were pretty sure she hadn't made a personal decision to follow Christ yet. Jill and I were tempted to discourage her from coming. We assumed she might find it overwhelming, and we knew the homework would be extremely challenging. To this day, I thank God that Morgan came. That first week, we discovered she needed a study Bible in a translation that was going to be easier for her to read. We purchased a new Bible for her and placed tabs in it to help ease some of her frustration in flipping from book to book.

Isaiah 55:11 reminds us, "So is my word that goes out from my mouth: It will not return to me empty, but will accomplish what I desire and achieve the purpose for which I sent it." Morgan heard God's Word during our time together. She may not have grasped every concept, but she grew, and she experienced the beauty of women studying God's Word together. I am so glad we didn't tell her she shouldn't come.

Encourage and expect your women to complete each week's homework. Set the bar high, but also extend grace when they fall short. Our women should never be made to feel less than because they didn't complete the homework for the week. Trust that God's Word will not return empty and that what they hear and what they do study will transform their hearts and souls. If we only offer milk, our women will never move on to the meat of Scripture (Heb. 5:12–14).

Training for Bible Study Facilitators and Teachers

When my family lived in Kentucky, I was invited to be a small group leader in an international, nondenominational community Bible study. Each week we attended a leaders' meeting where we reviewed the week's lesson in preparation for leading our group discussions the next day and also received intentional training. Some weeks we participated in role-playing exercises. Other weeks we worked through how to handle specific needs and situations. There was a level of accountability, community, and intentionality like none I had ever experienced. That experience forever changed my view of training and had a profound impact on how I led my Bible study group and related to my group members.

Many Bible study coordinators rely upon and rotate through the same Bible study leaders. Their list of solid, reliable leaders is short, but they aren't quite sure how to expand that list. Creating a process for recruiting and training new leaders is critical. I find many women say no because they don't have the skills, but they are willing to learn if given the opportunity. If you're not sure if your church offers training, ask! Sometimes, unintentionally, small group leaders receive training but women's Bible study leaders are forgotten.

Many churches are seeing the need to train up leaders and have begun offering in-house group leader training. Some churches:

- Purchase online training programs and require all new leaders to complete them.

- Offer apprentice-style training for leaders and require them to shadow and receive mentoring from another leader.
- Require new Bible study leaders to co-lead for one study with a seasoned leader.
- Place women's ministry team members in the Bible study class for support and encouragement.

Put a process in place to train your leaders, and you'll see your leaders and your groups flourish!

Competing with Online Bible Studies

In these post-COVID years, in-person church Bible studies are facing some tough competition from online Bible study offerings from other ministries and other churches. Many of your women may not differentiate between online and in-person relationships and gatherings. They find connection and fulfillment in both kinds of relationships.

Online Bible studies offer benefits that cannot be ignored, including convenience, flexibility, and the potential to interact with people around the globe. In today's overscheduled world, Bible study in pajamas at any time of the day can be a real draw for many women. Or, more practically, women may not have a Bible study option at their church that fits their schedule, perhaps due to work schedules or school drop-offs or pickups. Other issues like chronic illness, lack of childcare, and caring for elderly parents can also hamper in-person Bible studies.

On the flip side, there are some definite downsides to online Bible studies. They offer little accountability. Women who aren't participating can easily fall through the cracks. It's easy to turn off your camera, decide not to show up, or hide the fact that you didn't complete the homework. It's difficult to read body language online, and it's impossible to pass a tissue when tears start to fall. It's unlikely you'll serve in community together or be able to provide physical support in a crisis. Many online Bible studies break after the study ends, and leaders are unlikely to follow up or remain connected with each woman once they part ways. There's also the question of who's leading the study. What is their training and background? Do they align with your church's beliefs? My friend Joy also reminded me we never know who else is listening. Someone's spouse, child, or roommate may be in the room listening to the teaching and any shared prayer requests.

In-person Bible studies offer a different kind of community experience. Leaders can encourage members of the church to minister to one another during their group time and in the days between. (I'll share specific ideas for building community in chapter 6.) Leaders who fall under the authority of the local church will support the church's mission and beliefs. In-person groups provide opportunities to practice hospitality and fellowship at and between Bible study meetings. Leaders and members can follow up with one another and continue connecting long after the Bible study ends. Sitting face-to-face, leaders can read and address nonverbal cues that would otherwise remain hidden.

In-person Bible study at your church is ideal, but participating in an online Bible study offered through your church is still better than not attending at all. The goal should be to move women from online studies to in-person studies, with rare exceptions. If you have online Bible study groups, encourage them to meet in person at least once a month in addition to their online meetings. Our goal should always be to encourage our women to meet together as was modeled by the early church. Here is a list of Scripture to help you think through what is best for your women:

- Acts 2:42
- Colossians 3:16
- Hebrews 10:24–25
- 2 Timothy 4:3
- Matthew 28:19–20
- Titus 2:1–8

Removing Bible Study Barriers

If in-person Bible study is our goal, we'll need to take steps to remove the barriers keeping women from attending. What are the things preventing your women from coming to Bible study? Do they need childcare? Are you providing Bible studies at a time that is convenient for women in your church? I've got some ideas that will help you overcome the barriers of scheduling and childcare.

Creating a Bible Study Schedule That Works for All Women

Initially targeting stay-at-home moms, many women's Bible study programs of the past generations focused primarily, or solely, on daytime offerings. However, today we need to offer studies that meet the needs of all women, including working women, single women, and single moms, most of whom cannot attend the typical daytime Bible study. We need to widen our perspective and our Bible study schedules.

For over a year, one women's ministry team I served on prayed for God to clear the path so we could offer an evening study. Armed with a survey from our women that showed the need and desire for an evening study, we approached our senior pastor. He was quick to agree that this was a need but asked we hold off for the time being. He did not want to take away from the attendance of the current Wednesday night church program or create a situation where women had to choose which to attend.

As we waited and prayed, we saw God prepare the way for a women's evening Bible study. In addition to mixed discussion groups during that Wednesday night church program, the staff started to offer a women's only discussion group option, which was well received. Months later, the church staff decided to move away from Wednesday night programming, opening the door for the team to offer women's evening Bible studies at the church. The response was immediate and significant! A church with an average Sunday attendance of less than two hundred managed to draw thirty women to the evening Bible study, in addition to those twenty-five to thirty who attended the morning Bible study sessions.

It is important to make certain your Bible study schedule provides a variety of times and opportunities for women to attend. Take a survey to discover what days and times your women are available. While it's unlikely you'll be able to meet every single need, you'll see some obvious patterns of days and times that work for most. The women's ministry team at another church I attended offered five different women's Bible study options (same content, different times). One was very early in the morning, before most start their workday. Think outside the box!

Meeting the Need for Childcare

Childcare can also be a barrier to Bible study attendance. I know how very hard it is to find reliable childcare workers. I've been tasked with creating the schedule, recruiting the workers, and dealing with last-minute worker cancellations. The hard truth is that when we fail to provide childcare, we prohibit a large group of women from attending. Not everyone can afford a babysitter or has a spouse or family member able to watch the kids. Limiting childcare to preschool age and younger also leaves out homeschool moms.

Before you begin setting up childcare for your Bible studies, first have a conversation with your children's pastor or director. Find out what the guidelines are in your church for adult-to-child ratios at each age level and what training is required. Background checks should be required for everyone who works with children. Ask if they have a list of workers they can share with you (many do). Other sources for childcare workers include preschool substitute lists, teenagers (homeschoolers may be available during the daytime), retirees, childcare workers for local church moms' groups, and volunteers from within your Bible study.

It's best if you can find, or even hire, someone to coordinate childcare for your events and Bible studies. It is a massive undertaking, between finding workers and providing Bible-focused content for those in their care. Please pay your workers, unless they insist on volunteering. Paychecks encourage commitment. Gift cards or small presents at the end of each study are appreciated too. You may have to build childcare expenses into your budget or charge a small fee for the service. Don't forget to ask for donations if church policy allows. Most women, even if they don't need childcare, understand and appreciate the necessity.

What About Mentoring?

Where does mentoring fit in this discussion? Like small groups, mentoring is typically more focused on building relationships than on acquiring knowledge. You may have heard someone explain mentoring as "doing life together." The Bible has many examples of mentoring and discipling relationships, including Ruth and Naomi (Ruth 1–4), Mary and Elizabeth

(Luke 1:26–56), Moses and Joshua (Exod. 24:13; 33:11), and Eli and Samuel (1 Sam. 3).

Titus 2:3–5 is probably the passage most often referenced by fans of mentoring:

> Older women likewise are to be reverent in behavior, not slanderers or slaves to much wine. They are to teach what is good, and so train the young women to love their husbands and children, to be self-controlled, pure, working at home, kind, and submissive to their own husbands, that the word of God may not be reviled. (ESV)

Fans of discipleship also love Matthew 28:19–20:

> Therefore go and make disciples of all nations, baptizing them in the name of the Father and of the Son and of the Holy Spirit, and teaching them to obey everything I have commanded you. And surely I am with you always, to the very end of the age.

It isn't a matter of if we *should* disciple or mentor but *how* we should disciple or mentor. Traditionally, women's ministries have focused on both organic and intentional mentoring. In recent years, discipleship has edged out mentoring as a deeper, updated approach. As many churches embrace large-scale, churchwide discipleship programs, women's ministry leaders are left wondering what their role is.

What's the Difference?

Though you'll find some people use the two terms interchangeably, discipleship can be mentoring, but mentoring is not always discipleship. The differences may seem subtle, but as we prayerfully consider discipleship or mentoring as an arm of our women's ministry, we need to be intentional with our words. We need to decide which tool—discipleship or mentoring—will help us reach our goal.

Feeling confused? Until I did a little wrestling and some research, I was too. So many books have been written about discipleship and mentoring; I thought it best to look to the experts for our definitions.

Kandi Gallaty, in her book *Disciple Her: Using the Word, Work, & Wonder of God to Invest in Women*, defines discipleship as "intentionally equipping believers with the Word of God through accountable relationships empowered by the Holy Spirit in order to replicate faithful followers of Christ."[4] Melissa B. Kruger, author of *Growing Together: Taking Mentoring Beyond Small Talk and Prayer Requests*, defines mentoring as "a discipleship relationship that focuses on equipping younger believers for the work of the ministry, so that they may grow in maturity and unity in the faith with the ultimate goal of glorifying God."[5] You'll notice both definitions include intentional relationships with a focus on faith. Their aim and approach, however, are different. Discipleship uses the Word of God to equip believers to be faithful Christ-followers. There is also an additional focus on replication. Mentoring focuses on helping younger believers become more spiritually mature and glorify God. One could argue that the Bible tells us we are to do both: disciple and mentor others. The end goal is similar—spiritual maturity—but the approach is different.

To add some clarity to our discussion, I've crafted a chart that highlights the possible differences and similarities between mentoring and discipleship. You may find that your church or your own experience is more of a blend of the two.

	Mentoring	**Discipleship**
Time frame	May or may not have a specific end date	Has a definitive start and end date, often 12–18 months
Curriculum	May use a program or book as a guide	God's Word; may use a guided workbook or journal
Focus	Relationship and encouragement, spiritual growth through everyday life	Spiritual growth through the study of God's Word
Participants	Pairs a spiritually older woman with a spiritually younger woman	Most often occurs in small groups of five or fewer, can occur one-on-one, has a trained group leader
Approach	Usually organic	Organized, rarely organic
Frequency	May meet regularly, but may not	Meets regularly, usually weekly
Style	May be structured, but most likely not	Structured meetings, regular assignments
Goal	Guidance through a specific season, spiritual maturity	Spiritual growth and replication (disciples become leaders of discipleship groups)

The command is clear. We are to teach the next generation, but how do we discern which approach is best for our women? We need to prayerfully determine our goal. Is our goal to form relationships that focus on encouraging spiritual growth through everyday life? Or is our goal the regular reading of God's Word together in a small group over a period of time to develop disciples who will disciple others? Do we want an intentional, structured program, or an organic program?

Organic or Intentional

Within mentoring and discipleship, there are two different approaches: organic (informal) or intentional (formal). Organic mentoring and discipleship form most often out of an established relationship. A younger woman may ask an older woman if they could study a book of the Bible together or if she could offer biblical advice about a specific situation. Often, the relationship occurs without a verbal ask or a label. While they may decide to meet regularly, meetings are more fluid, as they are often "doing life together" and meeting as needed. Organic mentoring rarely uses a program or set of materials. No two organic mentoring or discipleship relationships will look the same.

Intentional mentoring and discipleship almost always use a format, a book, or a program. Women may fill out profiles and receive their mentoring match via email or at a mentoring launch event. Mentors and mentees in the program may follow a set schedule, use a reading plan, or complete a workbook together. Discipleship groups may be formed via personal invitation or registration, similar to a Bible study sign-up. Discipleship groups read the Bible together, sometimes focusing on a chapter each day or each week. Group members usually record answers or reflections in a journal or workbook, which are discussed during their weekly meeting time. Intentional mentoring and discipleship have a definitive start and end time, such as six, twelve, or eighteen months. Additionally, mentors and discipleship leaders often receive formal training and support.

For many years, I was a big proponent of organic mentoring, in part because I was on the giving and receiving end of it. Julie, whom I mentioned earlier, mentored me informally for many years. Lois, one of my prayer partners and friends, also served as an informal mentor. However, when my team tried to launch an organic mentoring program at one church, it was without success. Organic mentoring is challenging to implement as a ministry initiative. Ministry initiatives without regular guidance and encouragement rarely flourish. Intentional mentoring and discipleship ministry initiatives are more likely to provide the structure and accountability many women need.

Removing Barriers to Mentoring and Discipleship

Mentoring and discipleship programs can be intimidating! Often women feel they aren't godly enough, spiritual enough, prayerful enough, or fill-in-the-blank enough to be a mentor or discipleship group leader. The time commitment required can also be a deterrent. With overloaded schedules, the idea of meeting weekly (or even regularly) with another woman may not seem realistic or appealing.

As leaders, we can remind our women they have wisdom to share and that God doesn't require perfection. We're all still "under construction," but the lessons they've learned along the way can benefit the women behind them. We can remove these barriers by providing workshops or training sessions to equip potential mentors and discipleship leaders.

These three key trainings can empower your women to mentor or disciple:

1. Teach them how to read and study the Bible. This is something everyone can learn, and it is imperative that women are comfortable and confident in doing so if they are expected to encourage the spiritual growth of those God has put in their care.
2. Teach them how to pray out loud. Many of your women are probably not comfortable praying out loud. Share tools such as the ACTS (adoration, confession, thanksgiving, and supplication) prayer method and provide opportunities for them to practice.
3. Teach them how to tell their story. Encourage them to write down when Christ became their Lord and Savior. Help them share how God is making them more like Christ.

Providing training in these areas will prime the pump for a mentoring or discipleship program launch.

However, even with these efforts and our encouragement, not all our women will accept an invitation to be a part of a mentoring or a discipleship program. That's okay. As women mature spiritually, God will increase their desire to be in intentional, Spirit-driven community with one another. Pray fervently that God will draw those He desires to take part. We need to be faithful to invite women to participate, but their attendance is not in our control.

Rather than stress about the size of our groups or program, let's focus our energy and time on preparing and equipping our women so they can step with confidence into the role of mentor or discipleship leader when God calls them.

How to Launch a Mentoring or Discipleship Program

Chances are that discipleship or mentoring won't top the list of desired activities on your women's ministry survey. If God is leading you to launch a discipleship or mentoring program, you're going to need to:

- Introduce your women to the concept.
- Answer the question, "What's in it for me?"
- Train your leaders.

While it may seem unbiblical to market a ministry initiative, most of your women need a bit of encouragement—and many need full-out convincing! Provide the information in a winsome way and let the Holy Spirit do the calling and convicting.

Many years ago, one of the women's ministry teams I was serving on felt the Lord leading us to launch a mentoring program. We spent months praying. We formed a planning team that reviewed almost a dozen mentoring books and programs. We weighed the pros and cons of each, seeking what God wanted for our women. Once our selection was made, we scheduled a mentoring interest meeting.

Before that interest meeting, we introduced our women to the concept of mentoring at our annual women's ministry banquet. After our worship team sang "Side by Side," we invited three church members—Katlyn,

Joann, and Barbara—to share their personal experiences with mentoring. Katlyn, the youngest, was being mentored by Joann, and Joann was being mentored by Barbara, our senior saint. It was a beautiful picture of how we should pour into the lives of those coming up behind us and always seek wisdom from those ahead of us. Our theme for the year was "One Another," and God orchestrated it as only He could. Before our women left that evening, we announced the date and time of our mentoring interest meeting.

When my team launched women's discipleship groups in the church I currently attend, there was a three-week introduction class. During the first week, our women's ministry leader explained the purpose, cast the vision, and modeled the process. During the second week, we practiced the format together using a Scripture passage. Every participant completed an information sheet noting their availability so each could be assigned to a group before the next session. During the third week, each discipleship group leader led a table of women through a Scripture passage, and each group met briefly to decide where their first meeting would take place. If women wanted to be a part of a discipleship group, they were required to attend these introduction classes. The one downside to this process was that women had to wait a year to join a discipleship group if they missed the introductory classes.

There are many other ways to introduce mentoring or discipleship to your women. Workshops, kickoffs, book clubs, and Bible study books can all be used to gently introduce the idea of learning and growing together. Testimonies can also be an extremely powerful and persuasive way to convince women that it really does work and can be fun.

In addition to taking the time to properly launch your mentoring or discipleship initiative, you'll want to create a process and procedure for recruiting mentors and discipleship group leaders. As we discussed in chapter 3, just as members are recruited to the women's ministry team, these leadership positions should be approached with great intentionality and prayer. Invest time in training your leaders. Work through different scenarios and complete a sample lesson together. Help them get comfortable with the task ahead. If you're using a program or curriculum, make sure they have ample lead time to review it. Don't be discouraged by a small start! Seek to be obedient to God's leading and trust Him to grow the program in His perfect timing.

Assessing Your Bible Study, Discipleship, or Mentoring Program

If God leads you to implement a Bible study, discipleship, or mentoring program, it is incredibly beneficial to regularly assess its effectiveness. Are things working? Do you need to make some tweaks? Do you see spiritual growth? How will you measure it? Don't allow measuring spiritual growth to be a stumbling block. Pastor Robby Gallaty lays out five characteristics of a disciple in his book *MARCS of a Disciple: A Biblical Guide for Gauging Spiritual Growth*. These MARCS ask: Are members missional, accountable, reproducible, communal, and scriptural?[6] While spiritual growth is more difficult to assess than event attendance, with work, it is possible.

In addition, I encourage you to survey participants. Find out what their experience has been. You may want to assess their spiritual growth and the format of the program at the same time. Here are some sample survey questions:

- How would you rate your spiritual growth in the last six months?
- How would you rate your prayer life?
- How would you rate your confidence level in studying God's Word?
- How would you rate your sensitivity to the Holy Spirit?
- How would you rate your obedience to the Word of God?
- Describe any change in attitude you have had toward studying your Bible.
- Have other people mentioned noticing Christ at work in you? If so, how?
- What were your group leader's or mentor's strengths?
- What would you recommend we do differently next time?
- How did you benefit from the homework?

Review the feedback and prayerfully make any needed adjustments.

What Do Your Women Need?

The women in your church may not need weekly Bible studies, weekly small group opportunities, weekly discipleship groups, and weekly mentoring. Just one or two of those options may be what's best for them. Over time, you may find there's a need to add to or take away from what is being offered. Your church staff may limit or encourage you to expand the number of weekly options women have for engaging in God's Word and growing in relationship with one another. I don't know what's best for your local church community, but I know Someone who does! Pray and seek what the Lord's will is for the women in your church. Trust His timing.

Our women's ministry team prayed for over two years about how to add a mentoring or discipleship component to our calendar. We looked at several books and programs, but nothing seemed quite right. While we prayed, God was moving in the men's ministry. Though our hearts were ready, God had another plan in mind. Our discipleship pastor, Connor, ran a beta discipleship group with the men's ministry team (which my husband serves on). A few months later, he formally launched discipleship groups at the men's retreat. The men met in discipleship groups for well over a year before Pastor Connor asked our women's ministry director to implement the same program for the women in our church. She, along with two women on the team, went through the process themselves for a few months before launching the women's discipleship groups, as I shared about previously.

We have a biblical responsibility to make disciples who make disciples and to live out the directive to be Titus 2 women (older women teaching younger women). The format is up to you and your church leadership. Nancy DeMoss Wolgemuth, author of *Adorned: Living Out the Beauty of the Gospel Together*, offers this challenge to older women:

> We have to ask ourselves: Have we fulfilled our responsibility as an older woman? Have we modeled the beauty of an ordered life, lived under the control and lordship of Christ? Have we been faithful in reaching out to our younger sisters, teaching what is good, and training them to live a life that honors Him?[7]

I pray we'll be able to answer each of the questions with a resounding "Yes!"

Reflection Questions

1. Take the Bible study health assessment and record any areas of immediate concern below.

2. How does your team currently select Bible studies? Is there anything you would change about that process?

3. What is needed in your church: discipleship, mentoring, Bible study, or a combination?

4. What barriers do you see to Bible studies, mentoring, and discipleship in your church, and how could you overcome them?

5. What did you find most encouraging or challenging in this chapter?

Praying Through the Process

Lord Jesus, forgive us for anytime that we've failed our responsibility to teach and encourage our sisters in Christ. Give us the wisdom to know what discipleship or mentoring needs to look like in our ministry. Help us to find ways to encourage biblical sisterhood through our events and offerings. Amen.

Sample Accountability Questions for Discipleship

1. How has your personal time with God been this week? Have you been consistent in prayer and Bible reading?

2. Have your words built up or torn others down this week? Are there any changes you need to make to glorify God with your speech?

3. Is there an area of temptation or sin (including overindulgence, escape, addiction) that you need to confess and repent of? How can we pray and support you in overcoming it?

4. Have you been intentional about encouraging and discipling others around you? Is there anyone you feel called to reach out to and support?

5. How have you shared your faith this week? Do you feel you missed any opportunities to talk to people about the Lord?

Bible Study Habits

1. Place an "x" on the line at your level of biblical knowledge according to the scale below.

Preschooler — Elementary School — Bible Scholar

2. How often do you read your Bible?

_____ Never	_____ Once a month	_____ 2–3 times a week
_____ Only on Sundays	_____ 2–3 times a month	_____ Almost every day

3. What roadblocks do you face in reading your Bible? (Check all that apply.)

_____ Boring	_____ Don't understand it
_____ Too busy	_____ Struggle to believe it
_____ Not relevant	_____ Don't know where to begin
_____ Don't like to read	_____ Other _______________

Bible Study Habits

1. Place an "x" on the line at your level of biblical knowledge according to the scale below.

Preschooler — Elementary School — Bible Scholar

2. How often do you read your Bible?

_____ Never	_____ Once a month	_____ 2–3 times a week
_____ Only on Sundays	_____ 2–3 times a month	_____ Almost every day

3. What roadblocks do you face in reading your Bible? (Check all that apply.)

_____ Boring	_____ Don't understand it
_____ Too busy	_____ Struggle to believe it
_____ Not relevant	_____ Don't know where to begin
_____ Don't like to read	_____ Other _______________

Bible Study or Discipleship Health Assessment

As you respond, consider *all* the women in your church, not just those you see and interact with regularly.

How healthy is your Bible study or discipleship program?

1. Does your Bible study schedule meet the needs of all the women in your church?

   ☐ All ☐ Most ☐ Some ☐ None

2. Do you offer childcare for your Bible studies?

   ☐ All ☐ Most ☐ Some ☐ None

3. Do your women regularly read and study the Bible on their own?

   ☐ All ☐ Most ☐ Some ☐ None

4. Do your women understand and apply basic biblical truths?

   ☐ All ☐ Most ☐ Some ☐ None

5. Do your women have an overall understanding of the Bible from start to finish?

   ☐ All ☐ Most ☐ Some ☐ None

6. Does your discussion time challenge and encourage your women to grow spiritually?

   ☐ Yes ☐ No ☐ Probably not; it's rather short

7. Do you provide training for your Bible study group facilitators and teachers?

   ☐ Yes ☐ No ☐ Not Sure

8. Do your Bible study groups meet together regularly outside of their scheduled class time?

   ☐ All ☐ Most ☐ Some ☐ None

Make note below of the areas that might need a bit of attention or refinement.

Discussion Group Guidelines

Discussion groups allow participants to examine topics through the lens of the Bible. These guidelines will help you get the most out of your discussion group time.

1. Be on time.
2. Come prepared to learn and to share.
3. Be a good listener. Be patient and give others time to process and respond.
4. Be welcoming and encouraging to the other members in your group.
5. Respect different perspectives and opinions. Your group members may have come from a different church or background, but we are all sisters in Christ.
6. Pray for and keep confidential the prayer requests shared in your group.
7. Be willing to be transparent—with struggles in life and with this study. While at the same time, protect yourself and others by not oversharing and by limiting details.
8. Stay on topic. Keep your discussion focused on the passage being studied. Your facilitator is happy to answer other questions you may have outside of class.
9. Keep the focus on God and His Word by not bringing in outside material. Use Scripture or commentaries in your study time and discussion—not books, authors, or pastors—to support your answers. The goal is to learn more about God and learn to hear Him speak to you through the Bible.

FIVE

Planning with Purpose

Creating a Women's Ministry Menu

> They devoted themselves to the apostles' teaching and to fellowship, to the breaking of bread and to prayer.
>
> Acts 2:42

If you search for "women's ministry ideas" online or on social media, you'll find yourself surrounded by a seemingly endless buffet. There are lists of Bible study books, pages of ideas for seasonal fellowships, dozens of workshops you could host, hundreds of movie night suggestions, craft ideas galore, and more! There are so many things you *could* do, it's hard to decide *what* you should do. How can you sort out what's essential and what's not? How do you prepare a mouthwatering menu of activities and events that will satisfy the spiritual hunger of your women's souls?

No two women's ministry programs will look the same, but there are some things most ministries have in common. At the core of every program are Bible studies, which we have already discussed, and events. In this chapter, we'll dig deep and explore women's ministry event and meeting options. We'll also look at how often to gather and how to pay for these gatherings. I want to help you build a menu of options that's best for the women in your church. I'll help you conquer idea overwhelm and select events and activities that will help you create a thriving, Christ-focused women's ministry.

Remember that mission statement you crafted earlier, plus the five key women's ministry ingredients? You'll use those as a guide for every programming choice you make. Behind every activity and event placed on your women's ministry calendar, there must be a why. Why are you hosting this? What is your goal? How does it support your mission statement? How does it move women closer to Christ and each other? How are women learning to be prayer warriors, caregivers, theologians, evangelists, and disciple-makers?

Wisdom from the Word

When we gather with our women, what should we do? As we saw previously, the early church paints a picture of Christian life we can model: "They devoted themselves to the apostles' teaching and to fellowship, to the breaking of bread and to prayer" (Acts 2:42). This instruction comes immediately after Peter preached a convicting sermon to which three thousand people responded by repenting and becoming baptized (vv. 36–38). These people didn't return to life as normal. Instead, they gathered *daily*, devoting themselves to teaching, fellowship, the breaking of bread, and prayer. God's Word was their focus and anchored their time together. They were prayer warriors like Hannah (1 Sam. 1) and Anna (Luke 2). They were theologians like Mary (Luke 10). They were disciple-makers like Priscilla (Acts 18) and Lois and Eunice (2 Tim. 1). They were caregivers like Tabitha (Acts 9) and the Proverbs 31 woman. These new believers were committed to growing spiritually. Acts 2:46–47 describes these new converts as eating together "with glad and sincere hearts, praising God and enjoying the favor of all the people."

Don't miss the fact that once they received Christ, they changed their schedules and reoriented their lives to put God and others first. "And the Lord added to their number daily those who were being saved" (2:47). Their numbers grew because they were sharing the good news. They were evangelists like the women at the tomb (John 20) and the Samaritan woman at the well (John 4). The faith these three thousand exhibited impacted and changed their community!

Imagine the impact the women in your church could make on their community if people saw them as being faith-filled, dedicated to meeting together, growing in their knowledge of God's Word, and loving others well.

Ministry Memory

It was my first time overseeing the planning of the big table event at our church. God bless the team members who helped answer all of my questions. The big decisions had already been made. The date was set, the speaker had been selected, and by all accounts this should have been an easy task for me. It was an annual event that almost always sold out, and I had a bit of self-induced pressure to continue this successful streak.

I went over every detail with a fine-tooth comb to make sure we didn't miss a thing. As we reviewed the schedule for the event, I saw what looked to be a typo. The time set aside for the table hostesses to set up seemed a bit excessive from my vantage point. One of us would need to be at the church to unlock and lock the doors on Friday from 9:00 to 12:00 and 5:00 to 7:00, and again on Saturday from 9:00 to 12:00. While I could understand the need to accommodate different work schedules, did they *really* need that much time? I soon found out, yes, indeed they did. Most of the hostesses went to elaborate lengths to decorate their tables; several had been planning their decor and table theme from the moment last year's event ended. It was breathtaking, and no detail was overlooked. Chairs were covered and decked with bows. Handmade favors sat atop each plate, which sat atop a charger and a placemat. The centerpieces were unlike anything I had ever seen.

Women were known for showing up almost thirty minutes before the doors were set to open, and they didn't disappoint that year! There was no holding them back. They couldn't wait to get inside and admire all the beautiful tablescapes. I was thrilled to see such excitement about our biggest event of the year. Things seemed to be flowing smoothly, and the women were engaged and attentive for the first ten minutes that our speaker spoke.

As I pulled my Bible and notebook from my bag, I glanced about the room and noticed I couldn't see anyone else doing the same. I had come prepared to hear our speaker share her story and encouragement from God's Word. I didn't want to miss a word. Later that evening, as we were throwing away the trash and gathering up the decor, I overheard some women complaining that the speaker had talked too long. Little did they know that she'd actually finished about ten minutes early. Later, after a bit of reflection, I realized we came expecting two different things. I was ready to hear how God had carried our speaker through the sudden, tragic death of her husband, while those attendees were expecting a shorter and lighter message and loved every bit of the detailed decor.

Planning Women's Ministry Events

Besides offering women the opportunity to regularly engage with God's Word through Bible studies, small groups, or discipleship groups, most women's ministry teams host fellowships, meetings, or events several times a year. These events can be a great on-ramp into Bible study or discipleship groups and even church membership, if we are intentional.

You've probably heard someone mock women's ministry events as fluffy, shallow, or overly feminine. It's easy to brush off those remarks and think, *That's not our women's ministry*. Several years ago, I set out to gather some information about what women really think about women's ministry and surveyed over one thousand Christian women. When I asked what they thought about women's ministry events, these were some comments I received:

> "I feel like they go out of their way to be extra feminine . . . i.e., decor, topics. Just be normal."
>
> "I will never attend another fluffy tea party or spring mother/daughter type event with little to no spiritual nourishment. I despise this form of 'ministry' and feel it serves no purpose."
>
> "Cliques, focus on decor, shiny things, pomp and circumstance. I love things simple, pretty, and focused on Christ, not the color of the tablecloth."
>
> "Goofy women's events: I don't want to dress up in a poodle skirt and pretend to be a teen. Or wear pink boas and play children's

games. I'm fifty-five, not twelve. If I was doing it in children's ministry, that would be different."

"Boring."

"Primary focus on 'fun' and 'fluff' in order to attract attendance—everyone's time is valuable, everyone is busy, and her time should not be wasted on events that don't spur growth and change."

Ouch! I wish I could report that these comments were the exception and not the norm, but I can't. Repeatedly, women commented about over-the-top, ultrafeminine decor. They were tired of events that lacked depth and purpose. It's no wonder we're struggling to get women to show up!

Before you dismiss these comments as relevant only to other women's ministries at other churches, let me ask you a few hard questions (ones I've wrestled with myself):

- Does your team spend more time decorating for an event than praying for your event?
- If you have a speaker, how much of the schedule is dedicated to the message?
- When women talk about your events, what's the first thing they mention? Is it the decor?
- Do women bring a Bible to your events without prompting or reminders?
- Does every event you offer include the five key ingredients of prayer, care, theology, evangelism, and discipleship?

I'm concerned there's often a disconnect between the events many women's ministry teams offer and the wants and needs of the women they serve. Steeped in years of tradition, our senior saints may look forward to the annual tea and table events. Yet a glance around the room often reveals multiple generations are missing from the festivities. It's important we regularly assess the reach and effectiveness of our events.

While there is nothing wrong or unbiblical about tea parties or pink decorations, if our events lack depth and fail to spur the spiritual growth of our women, we have done them a great disservice. It's easy to get distracted by checklists, food choices, and pretty decorations and miss the purpose of our events.

Different Types of Events

I am so thankful God gives us the opportunity to minister through all sorts of creative ways! Meeting the needs of so many different women isn't a simple task, but it isn't impossible either. Offering a variety of ministry events ensures we meet the different needs of our women, keep our ministry from becoming stale, and create a more balanced schedule.

As you consider what to put on your women's ministry calendar of events, don't forget to include the five essential ingredients. Every event you host should include prayer, offer care for your women, help build them up with sound theology, invite them to become a follower of Christ, and encourage them to live out their faith. Some events may serve up a larger portion of one ingredient than the others. For example, a service-focused event is going to be heavy on care. Regardless of the type of event you're planning, strive to provide an opportunity for women to sample and experience prayer, care, theology, evangelism, and discipleship at every event. How you package these ingredients is what makes your menu unique.

You may find it helpful to categorize the types of events your team offers. A quick tally might reveal your offerings are heavy on fellowship and lacking in developing discipleship practices. Or you may find that the opposite is true, and your offerings are more often deep than not, providing few entry points for women who are not believers or are new Christians.

We can break down the different types of women's ministry events into five categories:

1. **Discipleship practices**: Women learn, experience, and practice a skill that enhances or encourages spiritual growth. Prayer, worship, meditating on God's Word, fasting, Bible study, and evangelism all fall under this umbrella. Possible event ideas include how to pray out loud, how to study the Bible, worship and prayer night, and how to share the gospel. Both in-house and professional teachers

can be used to deliver the content. The best events will include time for your women to apply and practice what they have learned.

2. **Biblical encouragement**: Women are encouraged by a teaching or testimony that highlights a characteristic of God (such as His faithfulness, providence, or presence) or a biblical truth. God's Word is central to the message, and the application of biblical truth is encouraged. Events offering biblical encouragement could include guest teachers or speakers, personal testimonies, speaker panels, and topical teachings—for example, a teaching about replacing worry with trusting God and a testimony about how God provided during a season of sickness or discouragement.

   Sharing stories of hope and healing can offer encouragement, but great care needs to be taken to keep the focus on spiritual transformation and Christ rather than emotions and the flesh. Consider asking your speaker for an outline of their talk to ensure the content and focus are in line with what your church teaches. If you're using a speaker panel, giving them the list of questions in advance will allow them to be more thoughtful in their responses.

3. **Practical skills**: Women learn, experience, and practice a practical skill. Survey your women to uncover what they'd like to learn. You may have women in your church who can teach these skills, or you may need to find a professional from the community. Examples of practical skills events include painting parties, organizing, fashion tips, flower arranging, knitting, budgeting, canning, bread making, marriage workshops, meal planning, and parenting workshops. Events that focus on a practical skill are often optimal outreach events.

   Whenever possible, content should be framed through the lens of the Bible. An easy way to add the gospel to a skill-based event is to have a woman share a testimony that ties in with the topic. For example, someone may have a relative who canned fruits and vegetables who also encouraged their faith. Another way to link the Bible to a skill-based event is to have a brief lesson on what the Bible has to say about the topic. What does the Bible say about budgeting? What does the Bible say about being a good steward?

I've found offering a choice between two workshops will expand your reach, especially if one is food-focused and might exclude women with allergies or dietary restrictions.

4. **Service**: While we want to encourage our women to serve in the community, offering opportunities at the church that connect women to the community is also beneficial. Invite a ministry partner to share briefly about what they do and conclude your time with a hands-on project that will support that ministry in a meaningful way. Ideas include making sandwiches for a local homeless ministry, no-sew fleece blankets for a women's shelter, pillowcase dresses to send with those going on a mission trip, notecards for local teachers, and snacks or care packages for emergency responders.
5. **Fellowship**: This may be the type of event you assume is the most popular based on past attendance. It may be tempting to offer more fellowship-focused events than others, but I want to discourage you from doing so. Offering too many could easily water down your mission: to share Christ and spur spiritual growth in your women. They should be sprinkled lightly throughout your schedule, not applied liberally. Women want events with depth, not just a calendar filled with social events.

   Fellowship events include game nights, potlucks, table events, holiday celebrations, and movie nights. They might appear secular at first glance but should always point women to the gospel. Sharing a testimony is an easy way to encourage women at these events to remind them of the hope and freedom that can be found in Christ.

It's quite possible you have an event that doesn't fit neatly into one of the categories above. Maybe it's a combination. That's okay! The goal is not to offer one of each type of event each quarter or every other month. We're not striving for an equal balance of different women's ministry event types but rather variety. Each event is a creative invitation to taste and see that the Lord is good.

How do we take these five types of women's ministry events and add in the five key ingredients of prayer, care, theology, evangelism, and discipleship? One of our most popular types of fellowship events is a game night, so let's use that as our example. In this scenario, the whole group will be playing bingo and enjoying a potluck of appetizers and desserts.

Prayer: Open and close the evening with a prayer, asking God to bless your conversation and time of fellowship.

Care: Your team warmly welcomes women in attendance with a table set up at the door at which they make a name tag.

Theology: Share a short truth from God's Word in a testimony or short teaching. Is there a woman on your team who can do a five-to-ten-minute teaching on 2 Timothy 2:5 or 1 Corinthians 9:24–27?

Evangelism: Tie the salvation message in with the testimony or devotional that is shared.

Discipleship: As you prepare to leave, challenge each woman to apply the testimony or teaching. Encourage them to take action and live out the truth they heard.

How could you apply the five key ingredients to a biblical encouragement event? Let's pretend a woman in your church is going to share a twenty-minute teaching on abiding in Christ based on John 15.

Prayer: Open and close in prayer. You may also want to add a time for women to share prayer requests at their table.

Care: In addition to the hospitality shown by the team, your women have been asked to bring donations of canned goods for a local food pantry.

Theology: Your speaker teaches from John 15.

Evangelism: Your speaker or another team member explains that to abide in Christ, you must have accepted Him as your Lord and Savior.

Discipleship: Women are given two or three discussion questions based on the teaching. At least one is an application question challenging them to put what they've learned into action.

What Women Want

At the beginning of this section, I highlighted what women said they *don't* want at women's ministry events. Check out these comments from that same survey about what they *do* want:

> "It needs to be a warm, friendly environment where women can be vulnerable and where Scripture is taught and applied to our hearts."
>
> "It must be spiritually inspiring, focused on pointing us to Jesus and then growing us in the Word. It must be joyful and loving. I must feel welcome and valued."
>
> "It is important that the Word of God is handled and presented accurately. It is also important that the atmosphere is loving and all-inclusive."
>
> "That it be welcoming to all women no matter where they are in their spiritual journey."
>
> "That the topic is presented intellectually and with gospel-centered/grace-based applications. Often, women's ministry [only] scratches the surface of being intellectually stimulating or academic but is very heartfelt. It would be nice to have both present and coexisting."
>
> "The event should be fun and engaging with activities that all ages can enjoy. I want those in attendance to leave the event with a desire to draw closer to the Lord."

Can you see how building your women's ministry event around the five key ministry ingredients will meet these desires?

Four Secrets to Great Women's Ministry Events

You're well on your way to whipping up a great calendar of events. These four secrets will help your team offer a five-star experience:

1. **Christ must be the cornerstone of every event.**
   God knows exactly what the women in your specific church need, but it is important to take the time to uncover it through

prayer and studying His Word. Before you search Google or scroll through Pinterest, seek the Lord's will. Can He use an event idea you've plucked from Pinterest or purchased online? Sure, He's God! But experience has taught me His ideas are always better than my own.

You must include Jesus at every event. Pointing women to Christ and encouraging their spiritual growth should both be a part of your mission statement. As you set your calendar, use your mission statement, the five key women's ministry ingredients, and your theme's Scripture verse as a plumb line for each event and activity. As your team members make suggestions, ask, "How does that event idea support our mission and encompass our theme for this year?" How will women be encouraged to become prayer warriors, caregivers, theologians, evangelists, and disciple-makers?

No matter what type of women's ministry event you have planned, you should always anchor every event with a verse or passage from Scripture. Anchoring your event with God's Word points women to Christ, communicates the importance of Scripture, and reminds them to view the event or activity through the lens of the Bible.

If your team is struggling to connect your event topic with God's Word, that's a red flag. Take time to examine the lack of connection and make any needed changes.

2. **Focus on spiritual transformation.**
Whether or not we intend to, creating events that intentionally elicit an emotional response from our women is manipulative. Feelings, though powerful, can be deceptive. We want God to transform the hearts of our women. Feelings ebb and flow. Our women need to learn to operate in the truth of God's Word and by the power of the Holy Spirit, often despite how they feel.

Our heart's desire should always be for our women to become more like Christ. We can encourage that process by creating events that offer an encounter with Jesus through the Word of God and inspire transformation. Ephesians 4:22–24 encourages each of us to put off the old self and put on the new one. We should be changing and growing! You may not always see new growth in others, but you have a responsibility to plant seeds and water them.

Always ask your team, How will women encounter Christ here? Answer this question both before and after the event. Reflect on how you saw God at work in your post-event evaluation (see the resources at the end of the chapter) so that your team remains focused on prioritizing God's Word and on opportunities for spiritual growth.

3. **Create an engaging and interactive plan for each event.** The best women's ministry events are interactive. As you plan your event, make sure you provide something for your women to do beyond grabbing a plate of food and taking part in an icebreaker. Get them up out of their seats and moving around the room.

   Ask them to:

   - Complete a task.
   - Respond (in writing or action).
   - Discuss the topic at their table.
   - Participate in a project.

Long lectures without discussion or interaction may discourage your women from returning. Placing them in circles instead of rows will naturally encourage discussion and connection. Provide an opportunity for your women to apply and practice what they have learned. Women don't just want to listen; they want to participate!

It is also important to have a time to discuss what was heard or experienced. Discussion solidifies and internalizes the message. Encourage your women to think about the message and what action God may prompt them to take in response. When we share those thoughts with others, suddenly there is accountability! Discussion groups help us become more comfortable sharing what God is doing in our lives. They provide space to request prayer, share how God has met a need in our life, or ask for advice on how to take action to combat a specific sin.

Consider using these three questions for the discussion groups at your next event:

- What did you hear that encouraged or challenged you?
- What did you hear that reinforced a teaching from the Bible?
- What action do you feel God wants you to take in response?

4. **Deliver every event or activity with excellence.**
Sometimes fancy decorations and theme-infused presentations are confused with excellence. Women are not judging your craft skills; they are measuring the depth of your teaching and thoroughness of preparation. My survey respondents were not shy to point out that they've been to events that were unorganized and lacking in purpose.
   I'll never forget the retreat I attended where the women's ministry leader apologized and admitted that she had thrown things together at the last minute. Unfortunately, that explained a lot of things we experienced that weekend. There was no excuse for her lack of planning. She'd failed to put a retreat planning team together and hadn't asked for help.
   Organization adds the polish to an event that will leave your women feeling valued and treasured. Take the time to figure out how much time each piece of your event requires and do your best to stick to the schedule. Recruit volunteers to execute necessary tasks. Prep your materials. So nothing is forgotten, tap your type-A teammates to work through the details. Handpick the person who will do most of the speaking. Enthusiasm and a sense of humor will help encourage your women to open up and participate. Time plus intentionality will yield an awesome event!

Event Checklist

As you review your event agenda, check to make sure you've included:

- **Prayer.** At the minimum, have an opening and closing prayer.
- **Announcements.** Present other opportunities for your women to grow and gather.

- **Icebreaker.** This provides an opportunity for women to connect, develop deeper relationships, and interact with women in the room they may not know or know well.
- **Testimony.** We need our women to share stories about what God is teaching them or doing in their lives.
- **Teaching.** This is related to the theme or spiritual focus or the activity directions.
- **Interaction.** Provide this either through a planned activity (craft, service project, skill, workshop) or small discussion groups.

How long should each event last? One and a half to two hours is usually sufficient for most monthly or quarterly events. Conferences and retreats will, of course, require additional time. Any shorter, and women won't feel it's worth their time to get ready and leave their home. Any longer, and women may struggle to find space in an already tight schedule. It's better they leave wishing they'd had another hour together than wishing the event had ended sooner!

Retreats and Conferences

Due to time constraints, women's ministry events often focus on surface level conversations, making it difficult to offer deeper biblical teaching. A retreat or conference can provide the time and space necessary to go deep theologically and relationally.

The women at the church I currently serve in greatly anticipate our annual fall retreat. We see a larger turnout at our retreat than any other event we'll offer in a calendar year. We travel about two hours to a retreat center in the North Carolina mountains for two nights (Friday–Sunday). Our schedule typically includes four teaching sessions spread across the weekend. We break at lunchtime on Saturday and encourage our women to go off-site for lunch and dinner. Women are welcome to take part in outdoor activities at the retreat center, hike in the nearby mountains, go shopping, or stay in and rest. We provide a list of suggested restaurants and shops. After each teaching session, we ask our women to move into an assigned multigenerational discussion group. We handpick women to serve as discussion group leaders to guide the conversation and pray. Each year, I love to watch how God deepens existing friendships and grows new ones. There are things our women can experience on this retreat we can't replicate on our church campus.

I've served in other churches that have offered women's ministry conferences. These were usually two-day events, including one evening and part of the next day, that focused on going deep into God's Word. Some included discussion groups, some incorporated service activities, and some offered a choice of breakout sessions. Some featured well-known Bible study teachers and were open to women in the community, while others were more of an on-site retreat.

Some of your women will prefer an in-town option, especially if they don't like to travel or prefer to sleep in their own bed. Others look forward to the opportunity to go out of town and experience new things. Both conferences and retreats are worth considering if your church staff are supportive. Typically retreat centers book out a year in advance (and give priority to groups that rebook), so you'll want to take that into consideration as you make plans.

Creating a Ministry Calendar

How often should you host women's ministry events and activities? This is one of the biggest questions women's ministry leaders struggle with. Leaders with small teams worry, rightfully so, about overtaxing their team members. How often is too often? How many events are enough? There's no one-size-fits-all magic formula, but you can craft a plan that is best for your ministry in your church. Take into consideration your team size, the church calendar, previous women's ministry calendars, and, most importantly, the Lord's leading. As tempting as it may be, resist the urge to copy the women's ministry calendar of another church.

If you're starting from scratch or relaunching a women's ministry, you may not have a precedent to follow or years of expectations that must be considered. As your team grows and God expands your ministry reach, you may be able to add more events and activities to your calendar. It's okay to start slow, and it's much better than burning your team out fast!

If you're part of an established team, I want to encourage you to pause before you plan the next ministry year. Check your offerings against the five types of women's ministry events earlier in this chapter, then consider these questions:

- Have you neglected working women by offering most of your events during the daytime?
- Does your calendar look the same as it did five years ago?
- Are your offerings a bit out of balance?
- Are there holes in your calendar the Lord wants you to fill?
- Are there some things you need to press pause on for the next year or for a season?

It's unlikely that a big overhaul is required, but some tweaking here and there might better serve your women. Prayerfully explore what, if any, changes God may be asking you to consider.

It can be tempting to plan one event or activity at a time, waiting until the event is over to plan the next thing. Despite the temptation to be laser-focused on the current event, there are a few flaws with that approach:

- Your team should always have an invitation to extend at the end of every event. What is coming next? When can women connect again?
- You risk losing momentum. Your women need to connect regularly to build and deepen relationships. Don't make them wait long periods between events or activities.
- You're at the mercy of the church calendar. When it comes to securing dates for events, the early bird gets the worm! You may find there are few available or preferable dates left on the church calendar for your next event.

Most teams find that securing dates on the calendar six months or a year in advance works best.

How Many Events Should You Host?

One women's ministry leader shared that her pastor only allowed them to host two women's ministry events per year. That's hard. It's difficult to build connections and deepen relationships when your women only see each other twice a year. I recommend, at minimum, four events per year. Try to space them equally throughout the calendar year. If a woman has to miss an event, you don't want her to have to wait months for another!

Not every event, though, needs to be big. If we look at Jesus's ministry, we'll see that He ministered to people on three different scales. First, we see Jesus teaching to large crowds. For example, Matthew 14:13–21 highlights Jesus feeding five thousand people, and Matthew 15:29–39 records Him feeding a crowd of four thousand. Like Jesus, we should host events for large groups. I recommend small to large churches (up to one thousand in weekend attendance) plan one big event per year, such as a retreat, special event, or conference. These big events almost always work best with six months to one year for planning with a separate planning team.

Second, Jesus ministered to smaller crowds. Matthew 4:23 tells us, "Jesus went throughout Galilee, teaching in their synagogues, proclaiming the good news of the kingdom, and healing every disease and sickness among the people." We should also host medium-sized events, ones that all women are invited to attend but don't require the large-scale planning of a big event. Medium-sized events include worship nights, special speakers, workshops, game nights, or service projects. There's still some prep work required, but you may not need a separate planning team.

And third, Jesus ministered to more intimate, small groups. He frequently gathered with the twelve disciples (Mark 3:14–19) and often with His team of three: Peter, James, and John (Mark 9:2; 14:33). We, too, should offer smaller group opportunities for our women. Bible study or discipleship groups encourage smaller groups of women to gather together. In-home events, such as potluck dinners or game nights, create opportunities for greater connection and intimacy.

Your church size will determine the number of large, medium, and small events you host. In a small church, all of your events may be geared toward small groups because you're still growing! In a megachurch (two thousand people or more), you're going to want to create opportunities for women to gather in different group sizes. And even within those big events, we want to allow women opportunities to gather in smaller groups by having them sit at tables or breaking into discussion groups. As you schedule events on your calendar, consider the expected attendance of each event and space them out accordingly.

Selecting the Best Date for an Event

Picking the best date for your women's ministry event can be tricky. While throwing a dart at a calendar may seem tempting, you can do better than that! Admittedly, there is no perfect date that will meet the needs of every woman in your church, but you can eliminate some poor choices.

I advise attacking this backward. First, exclude those dates that won't work. It's all about eliminating the competition. Don't give your women an easy excuse not to attend. Let's take a look at events, groups, and activities that might cause a conflict:

- Other ministries, such as the senior ministry, youth ministry, and choir.
- Large church events, including vacation Bible school (VBS) and the Christmas program (including setup and rehearsals).
- School vacation days; keep a copy of local school calendars to stay informed about these events.
- Holidays; even for events like Valentine's Day or Mother's Day, choosing a different day is best.
- Regular community activities, such as Friday night football games or the local balloon festival.
- Sports schedules; for example, if your city has an NFL stadium, avoid planning events during home games.

It will not be possible to eliminate every potential conflict. People are busy, and they will have to choose to come. However, you can make their choice easier by scheduling events when you know there will be fewer conflicts.

Additional calendar tips:

- If your church calendar isn't available online, ask your church secretary to send you a copy before your women's ministry meeting.

- Try to schedule events on different days of the week (unless it's a recurring event such as a weekly Bible study). If one of your women always works the Friday night shift at the hospital, she'll never be able to attend if you only hold events on Friday nights.
- May and December are especially tricky; Mother's Day and college and high school graduations will eliminate most weekends in May. December is often filled with church events and Christmas parties; early in the month or even late November may work better.

Before you place an event on the calendar, ask your team these three questions:

- Have we checked the church calendar?
- Have we checked the school calendar?
- What events might we be competing with?

Account for Planning Time

Bigger events usually require more planning time. Are you going to assemble a planning team? Will you need to search for a speaker? Will you need to secure a venue or a catering company? If you're booking a well-known speaker, you may need to secure the date more than a year in advance. Planning teams will need about six to nine months of lead time to organize a large event with excellence. While some people claim they work better under pressure, it is best to avoid creating a stressful planning situation. You want planning team members to share their excitement about the event with other women, not their complaints about how stressful or hurried the planning process has been.

God doesn't rush or hurry. He has a plan, and nothing He does is by accident. I try to remember these truths when event planning feels forced. The Lord is also quick to remind me of what happened when the team I was serving on was confronted with trying to plan a retreat in less than four months. Several summers ago, our team had to decide whether or not to continue with our annual plans for a fall retreat. We typically began planning about a year in advance, but this year the fall was quickly approaching and we were still without a date, location, or theme. Our team was divided on whether we should move forward. As we met and weighed our options, some members of our team grew more and more uncomfortable. There was pushback against the higher cost since we were unable to return to our previous retreat location. We were struggling to land on a verse or theme that everyone agreed on. Some other team members began to push and panic. If we were going to have our retreat that fall, we had to get stuff done *now*! There was a hurriedness about our approach that didn't seem right. Could we pull it off? Sure! But was that the best option for our women or our team?

After much prayer, phone calls, and some admittedly emotional conversations, we were finally able to come to a unanimous decision to host the retreat the following year, when we could take the time needed to make plans. Though everyone was not pleased, we agreed it was the right decision. God had several reasons for taking us through that decision-making process. Waiting a year gave us time to tour our top location picks and more easily secure a date. Also, working through conflict was good for our team. We were able to move forward united and confident that God used the no in that season for a yes in the next.

Should You Cancel?

Your event has been on the calendar for months, but sign-ups so far are disappointing. You're beginning to wonder, *Is it even worth it? Should we cancel?* Almost every leader has wrestled with what to do when it doesn't look as if there will be many women attending.

God knew in advance who would and would not show up. Our job is to be obedient and to carry out the tasks He's given us.

I'm assuming you prayed about this event before ever putting it on your church calendar. God knew in advance who would and would not show up. Our job is to be obedient and to carry out the tasks He's given us. I know this can be difficult when the numbers on paper cause us to panic.

Keep in mind:

- Women are typically slow to sign up for women's ministry events. Keep working every publicity angle and trust the numbers will come.

- Sometimes God is inviting you or your team to have faith and trust Him with the outcome.
- It isn't about the numbers. Sometimes it's about the one.
- Turn your panic into prayers. Maybe your team needs to be on their knees, praying for women to register.
- There are women who can't wait!

If you're tempted to cancel, please consider the women who will be disappointed if you do. I have been encouraged by leaders who have shared about the divine appointments and sweet times of prayer and encouragement they've had when only one or two women showed up. *Don't miss those moments!* Embrace the opportunity God has given you. Show those one or two women that they are valuable and are loved. God brought them there for a reason.

So, is it ever okay to cancel? Yes. You should cancel an event:

- If your pastor asks you to. Kindly ask questions, if necessary, but submit to authority (Heb. 13:17).
- If the weather makes travel dangerous. Make sure your women know how you'll communicate any weather-related cancellations.
- If continuing with the event would be a financial burden to the church. Get input from the pastoral staff and treasurer before making this call. There may be funds you are unaware of, or grace may be extended and a budget shortfall allowed.

If you have to cancel:

- Quickly confer with your team and enlist their help in communicating the cancellation.
- Use every communication means possible to spread the word—text, email, social media, website, and so forth. Hang a sign on the church door if you can.
- Refund any money if you can. If you cannot issue refunds, make sure you state that when women register.

- Cancel promptly, but not too early. Here in the South, for example, predictions and actual snowfall can vary widely. A forecast for a week out would never be a reason to cancel.
- Consider rescheduling, depending upon the type of event and the expected attendance.

Frequently communicate your weather cancellation plan if such cancellations are common in your area. One Bible study group I attended had the policy that if the city schools were closed, we would not meet. They always followed up with a reminder when we had to cancel, but at least it wasn't a surprise.

Should You Take a Summer Sabbatical?

In those early years of leading women's ministry, I looked forward to the summer with great anticipation. Our team would finally get a much-deserved break from hosting events and leading Bible studies. The first time a team member suggested hosting a summer Bible study, I pushed back. I didn't believe there would be much interest. I assumed women would want to take a summer break, but the sign-ups proved me wrong! Many of our Bible study regulars attended, but we also had a large group of teachers who were thrilled to join us for the summer.

A women's ministry leader in Alberta, Canada, had a similar experience. She approached a handful of ladies to ask if they could commit to one planning meeting in the spring and to lead one or two events over the summer. She ended up with eight awesome summer planning team members, providing a break for her regular women's ministry team. They brainstormed low-cost, low-prep, easy-to-drop-in activities. By the end of the summer, they had hosted one book club, two walks, a handful of park playdates, two fitness boot camps, a kayaking/firepit night, a board game night, a lawn game night, a prayer sister program, and a garden tea. They took turns setting up and hosting so that no one was overwhelmed. Each team member got to lead the event they were most interested in. They got such good feedback they planned to do it again the next summer with an addition of a service project and Bible study.

I know it can be tempting to take a break over the summer, but it may not be what's best for your team or your women. Women need Jesus in the summer just as much as they do the rest of the year! Many rely on Bible studies to keep them accountable and in the Word. Slower summer schedules often leave room for women to attend ministry events and activities. When other church ministries take a summer sabbatical, there is less on the church calendar to compete with. And those who are new to your church will be thrilled that they can get connected quickly. Summer breaks have the potential to greatly weaken or kill ministry momentum. Your women look forward to regularly connecting with other women in the church.

Another summer bonus is the opportunity to change things up a bit and test-drive new ideas. One church I attended hosted book clubs throughout June, July, and August. The church I currently serve in hosts six weeks of summer classes for women and men. This year there were eight different classes offered, most on Wednesday evenings. The optional potluck dinners forty-five minutes before the start of our classes were incredibly popular. Consider hosting a day at the lake, asking women to bring summer salads for a potluck supper, attending an outdoor concert, going kayaking, or offering an ice cream social. Invite women to take part in VBS for adults or go on a mission trip, host a block party at a nearby apartment complex, or hand out popsicles in a neighborhood next to the church. Embrace the opportunities the summer months bring.

While we shouldn't press pause on summer ministry activities, we also shouldn't take a break from our women's ministry team meetings—though it can be tempting! When my team failed to meet one summer, it negatively affected our biggest event of the year. Email and phone calls were not sufficient. We were short on time, and our planning was rushed. The registration team took the biggest hit because there wasn't time for sufficient training. We also failed to provide our publicity materials to the church staff in a timely manner. A summer meeting would have made a tremendous difference! If you are planning a fall women's ministry event of any kind, you should meet during the summer.

How to Work Within Your Budget

Now that you've filled your calendar with amazing opportunities for your women to engage with God's Word and each other, you need to figure out how to cover the costs. While it would be wonderful if every church budget included a generous line item for the women's ministry program, few do. If you're fortunate enough to have a budget, chances are your team is using their gifts to stretch it and supplement it. Most women's ministry programs are underfunded even though they may serve more people and host more events than other ministries (VBS, to name one) in the church. Thankfully, our value comes from Christ and not the percentage of the church budget we receive.

The reality is your team will almost certainly need to charge for events, solicit donations, or fundraise. Please check to see what is permitted in your church. These are not necessarily bad things, but procuring money for events will need to be factored into your plans. While some of your women may gladly donate needed items, that is an unfair expectation to put on future team members.

Charging for Women's Ministry Events

I know some of you are bristling at this idea, but hang in there with me. The church is one of the few places people expect events and activities to be free. Think about it. We pay for food at restaurants. We buy concert tickets. We even pay for parking. But church? No way.

We might assume charging for events will keep women away, but is that really true? When women invest in your event, even at the cost of $5, they are more likely to attend and more likely to participate. It's easy to skip an event that's free, as it costs the potential attendee absolutely nothing. Registering in advance and paying a small fee is a step of commitment.

Deciding whether to charge for an event or activity isn't always a straightforward yes or no answer. Let's walk through some things you'll want to keep in mind as you make this decision.

1. **What is your church's culture?** What is the expectation from the pastoral staff, as well as the congregation? Are love offering baskets the norm at events? Are you expected to use your budget for smaller events and only charge for bigger events? Does the church supply Bible study books, or do the attendees always pay? If your finance committee is unaware of the realistic cost of your ministry,

you may need to meet with them, prove your case, and respectfully request a budget increase.

2. **What are the income levels in your community?** Where I live, it's typical to see church members bring a cup of specialty coffee into the church service or Sunday school. Many families I know also grab lunch at a restaurant after church. So, it's reasonable to expect that charging them $5 or more for an event shouldn't be a burden. However, there may be church members for whom the cost of a retreat or conference would be a burden. Consider providing scholarships for women in need and invite women to cover the cost for a friend.
3. **What is the precedent?** When you've offered an event for free or at a price that is way under the actual cost, it can be really difficult to start charging or raise the price. For years, a church I attended was able to keep their retreats at a very minimal cost. They had been blessed by members with rental homes who had donated lodging, and then they had found a family-run hotel willing to slash their rates for our group. As the group grew and needed a dedicated meeting space, they were shocked when they researched conference and retreat centers and understood what the current rates were.
4. **What will the head count be?** Charging in advance for an event lets you know exactly how much food to purchase, how many programs to print, how many tables to set up, and so on. We are called to be good stewards, and it's difficult to do so when we do not know how many women plan to attend. Unfortunately, registration attempts for free events rarely mirror the actual attendance.
5. **Will attendees be open to personal investment in the event?** I prefer to offer a mix of free and paid women's ministry events. I don't mind asking women to bring food to a game night or to a fellowship event. And I prefer to request donations for supplies for a service project rather than to use our budget money. If we're hosting a couple of workshops, I'd rather charge for supplies than spend a sizable chunk of our budget. I always want the women's ministry budget to benefit the greatest number of women possible.

You may think that sounds great, but how do you figure out what to charge? At the first church I served as the women's ministry director, I was required to complete an event budgeting worksheet with our budget requests. Even if we weren't requesting money from the church, it was extremely helpful to figure out what we needed to charge attendees. Thinking through the nitty-gritty details helped ensure we didn't overlook a large expense or a bunch of small ones. I've tweaked and re-created this form for you to use. You'll find it at the end of the chapter in the resources section. Even if you don't have an official church budget, I still encourage you to use this form. The day may come when you're asked to show that the women's ministry should have a line in the church budget, and you'll be able to provide proof of how your team has faithfully stewarded money in the past.

Stretching Your Budget

Whether or not our ministry is blessed with a budget, we are all called to be good stewards of the funds we are given and collect. Make a note of the women in your church who love to hunt down bargains, and delegate specific shopping tasks to them when you can. I personally love the challenge of finding a great deal on items for a future event.

Five tips for stretching your budget:

1. Shop year-round for paper goods and decor for upcoming events. Red and green items purchased at after-Christmas sales can be used throughout the year.
2. Opt for potlucks over catering. Inviting women to contribute food not only keeps the cost down but can also boost your attendance. Many are happy to bring snacks, appetizers, and so forth.
3. Create and stick with a line-by-line budget for every event. Give each team member a set budget.
4. Invest in reusable decor items—lanterns, battery operated candles, glass vases, frames, platters, and so on.
5. Utilize in-house resources by printing posters, name tags, and programs at the church, as well as laminating and binding, if your church is capable of doing so. Only outsource what you must.

Favors, Door Prizes, and Food

Sticking with our metaphor of creating a women's ministry menu that satisfies the souls of our women, food and door prizes can add a nice touch, but they aren't essential for every event. If I'm being honest, women appreciate favors, door prizes, and food more if they don't have them at every event. It makes that extra effort and expense special instead of expected. If door prizes or food have become a distraction at your events, I am giving you permission to remove them. (You'll find tips later in this book about how to lovingly and gently make changes.)

What's typical in your church? Do your women expect big door prizes? Do your evening events typically include dinner? Have your women become accustomed to a take-home favor at every activity you offer? My team tends to pull out all the stops for our annual fall retreat. We've transitioned from retreat bags to table gifts at the start of each session. Here in the South, food is a part of most church events. We don't always provide a meal at our women's ministry events, but when we do, it's split between potlucks and catering. Last year, at our worship night in our pavilion, we invited women to purchase dinner from a food truck. That was a big time and budget saver!

If your budget allows for it, door prizes that point women toward Christ can be nice and even promote spiritual growth, but they are not necessary. Years ago, I put together my first basket of door prizes, filled with a variety of items that cost about $5 each. (Elaborate door prizes can be a distraction and source of envy.) This worked so well, I've created countless door prize baskets in the years since. I'm always on the lookout for sales and gather items throughout the year. I've included water bottles with a Scripture verse, trusted Christian books, verses on plaques, notepads, and pretty journals. Women were invited to choose one prize out of the basket, which increases the chance they will end up with something they want and will use.

We may think we have to offer food every time we gather. While certainly great discussions can occur while our women are enjoying a meal or a dessert together, we must take great care that spiritual food, not physical food, is our focus. It's okay not to offer food at every ministry event. Food often wreaks havoc on an already tight schedule. How do we keep our purpose at the forefront? One solution I've noticed in several churches is to ask women to arrive early or stay late to enjoy snacks outside of the main event space. For example, women are invited to arrive at 6:30 p.m. for a cupcake bar in the lobby before the event begins at 7:00. This method also may provide an easy out for those with food allergies and diet restrictions, who otherwise may not feel comfortable attending. Also, if at all possible, please make accommodations for dietary restrictions when you can. While these women may be used to not being able to eat at church events, the option to eat safe food will bless them.

Reflection Questions

1. How many events do you typically host in one year? Do you feel it's too few, too many, or exactly right?

2. Is Christ the cornerstone of every event your team offers? If not, how could your team rise to that challenge?

3. What could your team do to make your events more interactive?

4. How does your team decide if an event should be cancelled? If God is prompting you to reconsider that process, what might need to change?

5. How do you sense God may be leading your team to adjust your ministry calendar?

6. What did you find most encouraging or challenging in this chapter?

Praying Through the Process

Lord, thank You for the mission You've given our ministry. Please help our team to stay focused on that mission as we make plans. Please give us wisdom and discernment as we create our women's ministry calendars. Show us where we need to make adjustments in our event planning. Help us to plan events that will draw our women into a deeper relationship with You and each other. Amen.

Event Planning Form

Name and date of the event:

Event description:

- What biblical principle, Scripture passage, or verse is the focus?
- Who is the target audience?
- What is the purpose or goal of the event? How does it support our women's ministry mission statement? How does it incorporate the five key women's ministry ingredients (prayer, care, theology, evangelism, and discipleship)?
- How will women be encouraged to become more like Christ?
- How many volunteers are needed?
- What is the budget for the event?

Post-Event Evaluation Form

Name and date of the event:

Briefly describe the event:

- Who was your target audience? Who actually came?
- Was the attendance as expected? If not, why do you think that was the case?
- What was the purpose or goal of the event?
- How were women encouraged to become more like Christ?
- Describe how attendees were encouraged to become prayer warriors, caregivers, theologians, evangelists, and disciple-makers.
- How many volunteers were needed to organize the event?

- Briefly describe your promotion of the event:

- What expenses did you incur in connection with your event? (Itemize if possible.)

- What logistic information do you want to remember? (number of tables used, setup, menu, etc.)

- Would it be wise to attempt a similar event in the future?

- What would you do differently?

- What would remain the same?

- Briefly describe your impression of how well your event was received by those in attendance:

EVENT BUDGET WORKSHEET

Name of Event ______________________________

Purpose of Event ______________________________

Contact Person (Name and Contact Info) ______________________________

Event Dates ______________ Event Location ______________

Expected Attendance ______________ Approximate Cost per Person ______________

Fee Charged per Person to Cover Costs ______________________________

	Anticipated Expenses	Budgeted Amount
Pre-Event Planning		
Flyers/Signs/Banners		
Advertisements/Social Media		
T-shirts		
Other Promo Items		
Planning Supplies		
Food/Beverages		
Meeting Supplies		
Books/Other Resources		
Event Site		
Meeting Room Rental(s)		
Group Lodging		
Childcare		
Equipment Rental		
Decorations		
Cleanup Fees		
Tech Team		

	Anticipated Expenses	Budgeted Amount
Transportation		
Gas & Mileage		
Van/Bus Rental		
Guest Speakers		
Fee/Honorarium		
Travel & Transportation		
Lodging		
Meals		
Welcome Gift		
Worship Team/Musicians		
Fee/Honorarium		
Travel & Transportation		
Lodging		
Meals		
Welcome Gift		
Food		
Meal(s)		
Snacks		
Servers/Serving Fee		
Paper Products		
Other Expenses		
Activity Fees		
Programs & Pens		
Door Prizes		
Goodie Bags/Favors		
Name Tags		
Scholarships		
Miscellaneous		
Totals for Event		

Tips for Using the Event Budget Form

1. If your expenses do not equal the amount you've budgeted for the event, you're going to need to charge a fee, fundraise, or secure donations. Talk to your pastor about what is appropriate in your church.

2. If your ministry has no budget (I know that's the case for a lot of smaller churches) hold your planning team accountable for taking every expense into consideration, so no one spends money out of their own pocket to cover the cost.

3. Many of the items may not apply to smaller events. Just leave them blank and move on.

4. Use the empty spaces for expenses not already listed or place them in the miscellaneous category.

5. Submit a copy to your pastor and/or finance committee along with your annual budget request. Keep a copy for yourself and team leaders.

6. Consider adding a small miscellaneous line item to cover large events, such as a retreat or conference. A bigger event means there's a bigger chance you'll underestimate or forget a necessary expense.

7. Allow the team flexibility to move money from one category to another if everyone agrees.

8. Keep copies for future planning. It's a lot easier to pull out a retreat budget from two years ago and tweak it than to create one again from scratch.

9. Don't forget your servers and childcare volunteers. You may need to provide a meal for them, and you may wish to give them a small gift card as a token of appreciation.

SIX

Cultivating Community and Crushing Cliques

> And let us consider how we may spur one another on toward love and good deeds, not giving up meeting together, as some are in the habit of doing, but encouraging one another—and all the more as you see the Day approaching.
>
> Hebrews 10:24–25

For a season, my family attended a church where our efforts to serve were rebuffed repeatedly. It seemed from the outside looking in that unless you were in the "in crowd," your experience and ideas weren't wanted. The people at this church took the phrase "holy huddles" to a whole new level. The circles were tight. We never figured out a way in before God moved us out and to another church.

When you're on the team, it can be hard to remember what it feels like to sit on the outside of the circle. While that church experience was frustrating and discouraging at times, I'm thankful for it, as it allowed me to experience being on the outside. It's not a fun place to be. It's a feeling I want to remove from every women's ministry event. It is essential that the members of your ministry team crush the cliques and cultivate a healthy, Christlike community. Women are looking for connection. They want to be included. And if they can't easily find community in a church setting, they'll seek it out in other places. In this chapter, I'll share my best tips to help you cultivate community without creating cliques.

Wisdom from the Word

One of the most beautiful things about ministry to women is the blending together of women of all ages, stages, backgrounds, and experiences. The women in our church may be strikingly diverse, yet there is one thing that binds us all together: our belief in Christ Jesus. Our faith unites us and connects us. From the outside we may not look like members of the same family, but we are all sisters in Christ.

In a letter to the church in Galatia, the apostle Paul reminds them they are all one in Christ. Neither their gender, skin color, nor social standing could keep them outside of the family of God. "So in Christ Jesus you are all children of God through faith, for all of you who were baptized into Christ have clothed yourselves with Christ. There is neither Jew nor Gentile, neither slave nor free, nor is there male and female, for you are all one in Christ Jesus" (Gal. 3:26–28). We are one in Christ Jesus. Our faith is the basis for our unity. Our love for Christ creates community.

Satan loves to target the family of God. He plants wolves in the church. He tempts leaders to sin and deceive their flock. He stirs up division and pits church members against each other. He rejoices when gossip cloaked as prayer requests is spread throughout the congregation. Satan is determined to undermine the community of Christ. Our best defense against such schemes is a strong offense. How do we protect and maintain the unity of community? The writer of Hebrews has some encouragement and advice for us: "And let us consider how we may spur one another on toward love and good deeds, not giving up meeting together, as some are in the habit of doing, but encouraging one another—and all the more as you see the Day approaching" (10:24–25). The members of the body of Christ need one another. We need community with other believers. Not only do we need to continue to meet together physically, but our time should be marked by encouragement, love, and good deeds.

Ministry Memory

Sometimes our efforts to build community in our women's ministry can be met with resistance. As my team and I prepared to launch a new Bible study format one fall, I informed our Bible study coordinator, Sarah, that I planned to assign women to discussion groups instead of allowing women to choose their own group as we'd done the year before. Sarah looked me square in the eyes and told me that if I wanted to assign women to discussion groups, I would need to be the one to do it. Her strong reaction caught me off guard. I'd been in multiple assigned groups throughout my years in Bible studies at other churches, and I never remember it being a big deal. I'd watched women make new friends. There were so many times God put just the right women together in a group.

Sarah had her reasons. She told me about a situation several years earlier that had ended badly. There had been a couple of women who flat out refused to attend their assigned discussion groups because they did not want to be separated. Each week, as she would announce it was time to divide up into groups, these two women would slip off together to the same group. Gentle reminders to attend their assigned groups were met with tears and then hostility. Still nursing deep wounds, Sarah had no desire to get into a battle with anyone ever again over Bible study group assignments.

Despite her concerns, I moved forward with assigned groups that fall. We intentionally created multigenerational groups, and it wasn't long before we began to hear what a blessing that was. Our younger women were enjoying the wisdom from our senior saints. Our older women were inspired and reenergized by our younger women's excitement for God's Word. Women who would likely have never met if they'd picked their own groups developed sweet, new friendships.

Cultivating Community Without Creating Cliques

Did you know there's a loneliness epidemic? In May 2023, the US Surgeon General, Dr. Vivek Murthy, sounded the alarm on the devastating impact of loneliness and isolation in his Surgeon General's Advisory on Our Epidemic of Loneliness and Isolation: "Our epidemic of loneliness and isolation has been an underappreciated public health crisis that has harmed individual and societal health. Our relationships are a source of healing and well-being hiding in plain sight—one that can help us live healthier, more fulfilled, and more productive lives," he said.[1] Murthy also wrote that we must prioritize building social connections, and his advisory "lays out a framework for the United States to establish a National Strategy to Advance Social Connection" with six foundational pillars. The first pillar, Strengthen Social Infrastructure, includes "investing in institutions that bring people together."[2] The sixth pillar, Cultivate a Culture of Connection, stresses the importance of everyday relationships.

You and I can easily see how active participation in a church community, including women's ministry, can provide a real solution to this public health crisis. The women in our churches and communities are lonely. They long for genuine community.

In the survey mentioned earlier, the number-two complaint about women's ministry events—behind lack of depth—was cliques. Cliques are unfortunately common in churches and especially so in women's ministry. Whenever a group of women gather together, smaller groups are bound to form. As leaders, we want to see our women bond and new relationships form. But when those groups become, as defined by the *Cambridge Dictionary*, "a small group of people who spend their time together and do not welcome other people into that group,"[3] we have a problem.

How do we cultivate community without creating cliques? In this chapter, you'll find many ideas that will encourage your women to grow in their relationships with one another. We'll look at what it's like to be the new girl in the room and walk through some ways your team can intentionally create opportunities for connection and community. The most successful ministries will implement a multipronged approach delivered with love and consistency.

If cliques have become a stronghold in your ministry, be prepared for some pushback. Some of your women are happy and content with their clique and will see no need to change. I've heard countless stories of women who refused to follow directions and raised a stink when they were asked to separate from their friends. From tears to outright defiance, there's a much deeper heart issue at play here. Changing the culture is going to take time, prayer, and the Holy Spirit. While only God can change the hearts of our women, we can encourage diversity and issue frequent reminders.

We Were Created for Community

We are members of the family of God, created for community that meets regularly together, as Hebrews 10:24–25 reminds us. Christian community offers many benefits, including prayer support, sound teaching, encouragement, and opportunities to serve and use our spiritual gifts. Community with other followers of Christ also provides protection. Glenna Marshall, author of *Everyday Faithfulness*, says, "We put our souls in danger when we wander outside the safety of connectedness within the church and lose the truth of Scripture. The regular teaching and intake of Scripture in the community of faith protects us against falling away."[4] Christians rarely flourish in isolation. We're designed to need other people. Marshall also notes that "our spiritual growth both depends on and contributes to the growth of others."[5] We hold the cure for the loneliness epidemic.

Some of our women have lived without community for so long that they have forgotten its importance. Some have found community outside the church and may not realize what they are missing. Melissa Kruger explains, "The fellowship and care we have to offer one another is different from any other social group, club, or committee. Collectively, we're a body of people waiting together, looking forward to Christ's return. The church is a little taste of home in the midst of our journey through a foreign land."[6] It's up to us to set a good example and create places and spaces for them to experience community with one another, praying that over time women will see the beauty and benefits of Christian community.

Nine Ways to Build Community Quickly

We know there's a need, but how do we respond? Here are some tried-and-true tips:

1. **Pray for community.**
   I placed prayer in the number-one spot intentionally. Before we do anything, we should ask God to move in the hearts of our women. Pray for a greater concern for one another, sweet times of sharing, the breaking apart of cliques, and the formation of new friendships. Spend time on your own and as a team praying for God to

unify your women. Second Corinthians 13:11 is a great starting point: "Finally, brothers and sisters, rejoice! Strive for full restoration, encourage one another, be of one mind, live in peace. And the God of love and peace will be with you." You may also want to pray Colossians 3:14; 1 Corinthians 1:10; 1 Peter 3:8; and Ephesians 4:1–6.

2. **Engage in intentional icebreakers.**
   Before you or the women on your team roll your eyes, hear me out. I'm not talking about silly icebreaker games. Intentional icebreakers can provide quick points of connection when they highlight shared experiences and personal preferences. You can bet when Tammy discovers that Alma has traveled to Greece, her dream vacation destination, she'll continue that conversation later. Consider games that require women to circulate around the room and talk with others. Surface level, getting-to-know-you questions set the stage for going deeper.
3. **Pay attention to seating arrangements.**
   Assigned seating is a great way to ensure women from multiple generations interact with each other, and it removes that awkward "Where do I sit?" dilemma. However, most leaders bristle when I mention assigned seating—and I admit, I had to be sold on the idea too. One church I used to attend frequently used assigned seating at women's ministry events and even at some church events. Assigned seating was expected. Church leaders were intentional about placing people who did not know one another together and separating cliques. Seating arrangements were always created prayerfully and with grace, ensuring that women who brought guests were always seated together. Sometimes assignments were based on the area of town in which people lived. Table leaders were tasked with helping to facilitate the discussion and usually used icebreaker questions to launch the conversation.

   Whenever possible, I love to seat women at tables so they are facing one another. Circles signal conversations, while rows are best reserved for lectures. Most women I know aren't coming to a women's event to be talked to; they are coming to talk with others. Physically changing the direction the chairs face communicates this:

- The person on the stage is not the focus.
- The women sitting next to you desire and deserve your attention.
- There will be time to talk to one another.
- This is about "us," not about "you" and "me."

Depending on your space constraints and numbers, you may need to have your women sit in rows to listen to your speaker. Get them out of those rows and into circles (with or without tables) soon after the speaker finishes, so they can have a great discussion. There's something very impersonal about sitting in the back of the room looking toward the stage over row after row of the back of women's heads. As the pastor over small groups at my church says, "Life is better in circles."

If this idea is met with a substantial amount of resistance, you may need to take baby steps to get your group used to assigned seating. Start by placing sets of two or three table labels throughout the room. For example, you might use names from women in the Bible or seasonal images, and women can select from three different tables labeled "Martha" or "an acorn." This gives women an option of where to sit within those boundaries.

4. **Use name tags.**
   Yes, I know this sounds so basic, but I can't tell you how many times name tags are forgotten, or leaders think they are no longer needed. Being able to call someone by name builds connection and community. Help your sisters who struggle to remember names by using name tags at every event or activity. Use printed name tags when possible, so names are both legible and large enough to be read from across the table or the circle.
5. **Make introductions memorable.**
   I always write this on my agenda because it's so easy to forget! Make introductions more memorable (and increase points of connection) by asking everyone to share their answer to a quick

(not deep) icebreaker question. (You'll find thirty-one introduction icebreaker questions in the resource section at the end of this chapter.)

6. **Utilize discussion groups.**
   Discussion groups aren't just for Bible studies. Provide discussion questions for your women to answer after any speaker or teaching. Allow women to process and share what the speaker has discussed. Your women will grow in relationship with one another when they share their answers.

   Discussion group guidelines create a safe space where women can share without fear of gossip or judgment. You may find reading the guidelines out loud is sufficient for your group. However, if your group struggles with this, you may wish to provide a printed list.

7. **Have regular gatherings.**
   Community builds over time. There's no way around it! The more opportunities we provide for women to connect, the more connected they can be. Pray about how your team can provide consistent opportunities for women to connect.

8. **Host multiday events.**
   A larger chunk of time together will expedite community building too. Conferences, mission trips, and retreats that offer extended, focused time away from home provide multiple opportunities for connection and deepening relationships. The shared experiences—the speaker, the small group discussions, the meals, the late-night games, the service projects—will bond your women together.

9. **Share prayer requests.**
   Now, we're building community, not fear—so hear me out on this one. The most nonthreatening way I know of to share prayer requests and build community is to have women write one or two personal prayer requests on a note card and have them trade with another person at their table or in their group. For example, ask everyone to pass their card to the right. I beg you: please, please *don't* have everyone hold hands and stand in a circle. Holding hands, even if it happens to be someone you know, can be

extremely awkward for some of your women. For some it's too intimate a gesture, for others it provides a distraction from the prayer time. *Are my hands sweaty? I hope I don't catch her cold. How much longer are we going to stand here?* Save those prayer circles for times when you pray with your closest friends.

It's much more difficult to be catty with someone you've prayed for and who has prayed over you. Prayer softens hearts, opens the door for deeper relationships, and creates an intimacy that stretches beyond that moment.

When Women Resist Efforts to Build Community

Do you remember the Bible study group I mentioned at the beginning of this chapter? I wanted to divide the women into assigned groups, but it had gone badly in the past. As the new girl on the team, I used that to my advantage. I didn't have a history with these women, and to their knowledge, I did not know this had been a problem in the past. I was prepared for a bit of pushback but prayed it wouldn't happen.

At our intro week of Bible study that fall, I shared with our group of about thirty-five women that we would divide them up into three smaller groups. We asked each one to fill out an information card and note their decade (twenties, thirties, forties, fifties, sixties, and so on) on the top right corner of their card. I explained that after our time together, our group leaders would meet to pray over the cards and ask the Lord to arrange our groups. I shared my experiences of how God had repeatedly placed me in just the right Bible study groups without fail. Knowing how anxious some of them would be, we promised to have their group leader email them promptly.

When we formed our Bible study groups later that morning:

- We paperclipped the cards of church members with the guest they had invited to the study so they would be assigned to the same group.
- We divided our cards into piles by decade so we could form multi-generational groups.

- We shuffled each pile of cards and flipped them upside down so we couldn't see the names.
- We prayed and asked the Lord to place our women where He wanted them.
- We had each group leader take turns drawing one card from a pile until no cards remained, then they moved to the next decade. Our goal was to balance the groups so that all ages were represented equally. Once all the cards had been distributed, each group leader flipped her cards over and prayerfully examined her group.
- We looked for known conflicts (for example, an ex-wife and current wife or another situation that might cause division) and adjusted the groups accordingly. We tried very hard not to alter the groups the Lord created unless we all agreed it was necessary.

I have no doubt some of our women were disappointed they were in a different group from one or more of their friends, but they were welcome to socialize before class and sit together during our opening, and they could visit again after our discussion group time. At the end of the study, we had many comments from our women on our survey that they loved having a wide variety of ages in their group. In time, they made new friends and discovered the beauty of learning together.

While I pray your women warmly receive your efforts to cultivate community in your church, I know that's not always going to be the case. Don't let a few grumbles or groans keep you from moving forward with plans to bust up cliques. Refuse to take part in or tolerate poor behavior. You may have to pull another woman aside to lovingly discuss her attitude or actions. Assume she wasn't aware, and pray for her. If a one-on-one meeting doesn't yield results, I encourage you to seek godly counsel. A meeting with your pastor may be necessary and can help you determine the best way to manage that specific situation.

Over time, most will tire of instigating or complaining and may even see the benefit of getting to know other women in the church. Highlight new friendships when you can. Invite women to share how they've seen God's provision in placing them in their discussion group for Bible study or at a retreat.

When my family moved to Kentucky for a season, God placed me and two other new residents—in a town with few transplants—in the same community Bible study discussion group. We became like the three musketeers, spending many days exploring our new town, experiencing new restaurants together, and uncovering treasures in nearby thrift stores. Adapting to our new community with others helped to pull me out of the depression I had fallen into after our move. I have no doubt God orchestrated the arrangement so we could have a built-in support system to help each one of us adjust.

Model community. Encourage community. Talk about community. Lead a retreat or Bible study on community and hospitality. Share verses with your women that speak to community and unity on social media. Add community to your group prayers. You don't have to annoy your women with reminders, but God can use the sprinkling of community-minded words and thoughts to change their hearts.

Welcoming Guests

Because of extenuating circumstances and multiple moves, our family has had the opportunity to visit well over a dozen different churches. It's been my least favorite part about moving. We tried to narrow the field by investigating each church online first. Once we decided to attend, we did so with the intent of staying. However, with two boys in tow, we gave each church one chance to make a good first impression. If things didn't go well, we weren't likely to return.

Some of the churches we've visited were less friendly than others. We might be welcomed at the door, but once we found a place to sit, it was rare for anyone to approach us before or after the church service. Did no one notice a new family sitting nearby? Feeling unwelcome at a Sunday morning service or a women's ministry event is not uncommon. As Thom S. Rainer points out in *Becoming a Welcoming Church*, "Many church leaders and members think their churches are healthier than they really are. Many leaders and members think their churches have better ministries than they really do. And many leaders think their churches are friendlier than they really are."[7] I'm sure they thought the welcome team greeting us at the door would make us feel welcome. It did, but only for a moment. Once we sat down in the sanctuary, the silence hit us hard. Glancing around the room at church members hugging and chatting made us feel even more isolated and unwelcome. Thankfully, not every experience we've had has been disappointing.

At one church, after three Sundays of visiting "under the radar," we completed and submitted the all-important visitor form. We checked the boxes of several ministries we were interested in knowing more about. Youth ministry. Check. Men's ministry. Check. Women's ministry. Check. We'd jumped through these hoops at other churches, often receiving little or no follow-up from ministry leaders. To be honest, we'd learned to keep our expectations low. Thank God this church was different! I must admit, I was pleasantly surprised to receive an email from the women's ministry director.

In her warm and welcoming email, she:

- Let me know where I could find women's ministry news and info.
- Asked if I'd like to be included in the online women's ministry communication.
- Noted she was aware I had already signed up for the next Bible study session.
- Gracefully wove in the mission and purpose of their women's ministry.
- Included details and an invitation to the next women's ministry event.
- Invited me to contact her with any questions I had.

I felt welcomed! And in case you're wondering, she didn't know that I had an online ministry for women's ministry leaders.

There's a fine line between making someone feel welcome and overwhelming them. Develop and implement a plan to ensure that unfamiliar faces are greeted warmly and introduced individually to others at every women's ministry event.

I've attended women's ministry events as the new girl and did not have a single person approach me or welcome me. Unfortunately, I am not alone in this experience. Rainer explains, "Churches perceive they are a friendly church because the members are friendly to one another. But they don't think about walking in the shoes of first-time guests."[8] Your women probably are very friendly to the women they know, but they may not be so friendly to those they don't know. I'm sure they don't *mean* to come off as unfriendly. They may be so busy catching up with friends they haven't seen recently that they overlook the first-time guests in the room.

Include community building in your leadership training for all of your team members and volunteers. Don't assume women know how to be welcoming. Train them to make purposeful introductions and to engage women they see sitting on the sidelines. Help them be aware of times they slip into holy huddles and cliques. Consider role-playing different situations so they can practice. Your ministry team needs to model what they expect from those in attendance. If you don't want your leaders to huddle and chat in the kitchen once women arrive, then tell them in advance you expect them to circulate and talk to women they don't know well. Showing what you expect is powerful and eliminates questions and assumptions.

Quick Tips for Your Team

- Listen and ask questions. Sometimes we smother guests with talk about ourselves or the church. Get to know your guests. Identify *their* needs.
- Don't dismiss those who aren't new in town. They may not be as connected as you may assume.
- Warmly greet your women in the parking lot near the door you want them to enter. Many of them won't know which door they should use.
- Use ushers to help guests find an empty chair if this might be a crowded event. It's super awkward to wander around looking for a space to sit.
- Before your event begins, share where the bathrooms are located and how best to get to them.
- Explain everything. If you want participants to stand or sit down, tell them. If you're going to move to another room, explain how they'll get there and what they need to do when they arrive.

- Position greeters inside your event space, not just at the door. Train those greeters to look out for and connect women with others in a similar season of life or with similar aged children.
- Provide words for every song you sing. Use the screen, your programs, or both.
- Never assume prior knowledge of a biblical book, character, or concept. Always give background and context.

As a first-time guest, it can be a challenge to figure out who is part of the event and who isn't. Purchase shirts for your team to wear, place stickers on name tags, or use unique lanyards to help leaders stand out in the crowd. Do everything possible to make every woman feel welcome.

Is Your Team a Clique?

In some churches, the women's ministry team is a clique. Do your women see you as a tight-knit group that's hard to break into? Do you travel together in a pack? Do you fail to include women outside of the team in your event planning or implementation? Are the faces seen on the stage or in the front of the room the same month after month and year after year? What can you do to change any perception that your team is a clique?

Every step we take to combat cliques by cultivating community is worth it. We all long to belong. Women who feel included can't wait to return to the next Bible study or ministry event with a friend in tow.

Encourage Community Beyond Bible Study

Jill's invitation to grab lunch after our first Bible study meeting meant more to me than she'll ever know. Her invitation was a lifeline to my depressed soul. I was desperate for community! My family had moved from North Carolina to Kentucky in early July, when the heat kept everyone indoors or sent them splashing in the pool. I'd met only a few people, and I was aching to connect with some other moms.

Over the years, I've had the opportunity to be a part of Bible studies that encouraged community and others that did not. I've witnessed the change in dynamics and greater depth of sharing that can happen when women build relationships beyond the one or two hours they are in Bible study together.

In one church, the leaders scheduled regular, optional lunches every other week. Group members were emailed in advance with the date and location, with every effort made to select restaurants that were child-friendly and affordable. At the community Bible study, childcare arrangements were made about four times per year so we could meet thirty minutes early for a light breakfast and fellowship. In alternating months, we'd gather at a group member's home after Bible study for fellowship and bagged lunches. Our host would provide drinks and dessert. Holiday parties and service projects are also great ways to build community among Bible study members.

We can also encourage community when we leave the door open for women to join our Bible study groups after the initial start date. Women aren't going to wait around for our Bible studies to open up again; they are going to go elsewhere. We know God can use even one week in the Bible study group to whet a woman's appetite to sign up for the next study. Let's say yes when women ask if there are any openings in our Bible study groups.

We know God can use even one week in the Bible study group to whet a woman's appetite to sign up for the next study.

As Bible study leaders, we can build relationships and community by connecting one-on-one with group members between meetings. In addition to weekly email reminders to the whole group (homework reminders, words of encouragement, weekly announcements), I recommend leaders take time to connect with at least a third of their group members each week via a personal phone call, text, email, or a handwritten note. Reach out to women who were absent and let them know they were missed. Follow up with the answer to a question that Avery asked. Thank Felicia for sharing what God revealed to her through the lesson that week. Pray with Camden as she seeks to minister to her ailing mother. Those small touches will build community.

The Necessity of Volunteers

Everywhere I've served, and even in places where I haven't, I've seen this women's ministry mistake. And I'm not just throwing stones; I'm guilty of committing it myself. One of the biggest mistakes women's ministry teams make *is not using women outside of the women's ministry team.* This one mistake can:

- Increase burnout.
- Dismiss the other women in the church.
- Fuel pride.
- Create isolation.

I've been a part of and witnessed teams that do it all themselves. Whether it's an issue of assuming other women are too busy; not making the time to make a few phone calls, texts, or emails; or hanging on to control, it's a problem. When we exclude women of the church from serving at our women's ministry events, we can:

- Create a clique.
- Keep women from using their God-given gifts (1 Pet. 4:10).
- Restrict other women from being a blessing.
- Inadvertently hurt others' feelings.
- Limit our reach.

Look for places and ways your team can invite other women to serve. For example, food and hospitality are easy places to plug in volunteers. When we ask women outside of our ministry team to serve, it does three things:

1. **It allows other women to use their God-given gifts.** Women who are gifted in hospitality may jump at the opportunity to bring food or welcome women at your next event.
2. **It can increase your attendance.** If women bring a dish or serve on the welcoming team, it guarantees they will show up, and chances are they will bring a few friends along with them. If you are

struggling to get a specific generation to come to your events, ask them to bring some food or serve.

3. **It gives your team a break.** Seriously. Your team is already working hard to pull off the event. They don't need to be the ones making food and greeting women at the door for every single event. They are doing enough.

Tap some women who are welcoming to serve as hostesses. Call on some mighty prayer warriors to serve as prayer counselors. Then, when it's time to add women to your team, you'll have a whole pool of women whose strengths you know and who have already dipped their toes into women's ministry.

The time you invest in creating community and crushing cliques is worth it. The health of your women's ministry depends on it.

Reflection Questions

1. To what degree are cliques an issue in your church?

2. What's one thing you could do to cultivate community at your next women's ministry event or activity?

3. What is your process for welcoming first-time guests? If there isn't one in place, what are some things you think it should include?

4. What did you find most encouraging or challenging in this chapter?

Praying Through the Process

Lord, help us to create a community for our women that draws them closer to one another and closer to You. Help us to warmly welcome guests. Please break apart any cliques that have formed among our women. Help us to love one another well. Amen.

Thirty-One Introduction Icebreaker Questions

1. If money were no object, what would you do with your life?
2. What's one of your pet peeves?
3. If you could host a talk show, who would be your first guest?
4. What are you most passionate about?
5. What is your favorite thing to spend money on?
6. What is your favorite color, and how does that color make you feel?
7. Which household chore do you dread the most?
8. What's your favorite time of day and why?
9. What's one movie you could watch forever on repeat?
10. What are three of your favorite foods?
11. What is your favorite outdoor activity?
12. If finances and time were not an object, what hobby would you adopt and why?
13. What is a favorite memory you have from high school?
14. What was your favorite class in school and why?
15. Share one thing you love to do that you get to do nearly every day.
16. What is one important skill every person should master?
17. What is your favorite local restaurant and the meal you most enjoy there?
18. If you could live in any sitcom, which one would it be?
19. How would you spend a million dollars?
20. What are two things you consider yourself to be very good at?
21. What's the best dessert you've ever had?
22. What are your three favorite smells?
23. If you were in the Miss America competition, what would your talent be?
24. If you had one extra hour of free time a day, how would you use it?

25. When was the last time you did something for the first time? What was it?
26. If you could be anywhere, doing anything right now, where would you be and what would you be doing?
27. If you joined the circus, what act would you most want to perform?
28. What aspect of your daily routine do you look forward to the most?
29. What is your favorite day of the year?
30. What is something you have that is of sentimental value?
31. What one modern convenience could you not live without?

SEVEN

Engaging in Missions, Service Projects, and Evangelism

> Therefore go and make disciples of all nations, baptizing them in the name of the Father and of the Son and of the Holy Spirit, and teaching them to obey everything I have commanded you. And surely I am with you always, to the very end of the age.
>
> Matthew 28:19–20

Sometimes we get so focused on building community *inside* the church that we forget God also calls us to bring those *outside* of the church into community with Him. Caring for the souls of the lost is at the heart of evangelism. In this chapter, we'll dive deeper into the two essential women's ministry ingredients of care and evangelism. How does God want us to care for others? How can we invite and encourage our women to serve others?

We'll start with a look at what God's Word says, and then we'll unpack the difference between missions, service projects, outreach, and evangelism. I'll share how God used a simple service project to launch a new ministry outreach, plus provide tips for nurturing missions-minded women and building relationships with parachurch ministries. We'll also discuss some simple ways to add these ideas to your women's ministry events and meetings.

Wisdom from the Word

What does God's Word have to say about missions, outreach, service projects, and evangelism? As we saw in chapter 2, God provides examples in Scripture of women who were caregivers and evangelists. Additionally, Jesus gives a clear command to share the good news and sets an example of serving others.

The Samaritan woman at the well left her water jar and went and told the people in the town about Jesus (John 4:28–29). After the women discovered Jesus's empty tomb, they immediately went and told the disciples what they had seen (Luke 24:1–10). Why the urgency? Did they understand, as we do, that Jesus is coming back and that those who do not know Him will perish?

When Jesus visited with the eleven disciples after His resurrection, He gave them very specific instructions: "Go and make disciples of all nations, baptizing them in the name of the Father and of the Son and of the Holy Spirit, and teaching them to obey everything I have commanded you" (Matt. 28:19–20). With the Holy Spirit as their guide, the disciples were commanded to go and make more disciples. This command extends to all believers. We each have a responsibility—a mission, if you will—to share the good news.

You may recall Tabitha (Acts 9), Lydia (Acts 16), and the Proverbs 31 woman are biblical examples of caregivers. Tabitha and the Proverbs 31 woman actively served the poor, and Lydia opened her home to serve others. We are to do the same.

Jesus modeled the importance of serving others as He washed His disciples' feet. At first, the disciples were confused. Simon Peter even asked Jesus to wash his head too. Jesus removed their confusion when He said, "I have set you an example that you should do as I have done for you. Very truly I tell you, no servant is greater than his master, nor is a messenger greater than the one who sent him. Now that you know these things, you will be blessed if you do them" (John 13:15–17). When we serve others, we follow the example Jesus set.

Ministry Memory

I'm still in awe over the things God did through our partnership with a local women's shelter. The time we spent with the women and children there was precious. Many of the women had few belongings, so being able to give them a handmade blanket or nail polish and some makeup was a big deal. It's hard for me to put it into words, but there was something holy and special about every outreach we planned for that shelter. We continuously saw God at work in ways that made us eager to do more.

The address of the shelter was carefully guarded to protect the women and children who had escaped from abusive situations, so it wasn't possible to have food delivered. When one of our team members went to pick up pizza for lunch one day, somehow the girl at the pizza place figured out where we were taking it. She shared that she could have delivered it for us. She knew the address because she'd once stayed there. Then there was a particular woman who helped us provide an afternoon of pampering. She wasn't a member of our church, and I can't remember who gave us her name, but for some reason God made sure we connected. I shared our desire to provide an afternoon of pampering for the women at a nearby shelter, and for a moment she went silent on the phone. Then she began to share with me that she knew exactly where it was, as she, too, had spent some time living there. She was honored to be able to go back and give back in a small way.

God continued to connect us with women who had stayed in that shelter, but one in particular caught us by surprise. Tears rolled down the faces of each member of our women's ministry team as they learned that Laura, one member of our team, had once lived in the shelter too. She was hesitant to share her story with us because she had a family now, and few people knew the details. Our hearts were tender toward the women and children who had sought refuge from abusive situations, but their stories seemed distant from our comfortable and safe homes until we learned one of our own had sought shelter there too. As we wiped away the tears, it was clear to each one of us God's divine providence had led us to form a partnership with that shelter.

What Is the Difference?

Much like there is an overlap between discipleship, Bible study, and mentoring, there is also an overlap between how we define missions, service projects, outreach, and evangelism. They can have similar focuses and outcomes, but there are slight differences. I'll unpack how I view the differences below, but it will serve you well to understand the philosophy and terminology used by your church staff.

Just as you may have a discipleship pastor in your church whom you need to support and complement, you may also have a missions pastor to support and complement. Your church could even have a separate women's ministry missions team (for example, Women on Mission). Regardless of other directors, teams, or committees in your church that already focus on missions, service, outreach, and evangelism, God's Word is clear *everyone* is to serve others and share the gospel (Matt. 28:19–20). Robust biblical discipleship will result in a desire to serve others and tell them about Christ.

Before we begin, we need to define our terms. *Mission* can be used as a verb and an adjective. Typically, missions are planned trips or activities outside of the church focused on reaching unbelievers and sharing the gospel. Examples include mission trips to unreached people groups inside and outside of the country. Mission is also often used to describe the way we live our lives as Christians. I've heard many pastors remark that "We are all on mission," meaning that we should all be looking to share the gospel with unbelievers. As the *Holman Bible Dictionary* points out, "Interestingly, the term mission is not found in the Scriptures, yet the concept of mission permeates the entire Bible."[1] As women's ministry leaders, we might organize prayer for missionaries, invite women to go on a mission trip, or support mission trips through the collection of monetary donations or supplies. Perhaps you'll even host a women's mission trip to serve alongside missionaries stationed in another community or country.

Service projects are typically projects in the community or for the community that meet a practical or physical need (for example, landscaping at a parachurch ministry, collecting diapers for a pregnancy center, or baking and taking cookies to first responders). Service projects often include fellowship opportunities for church members as they serve side by side working on a project. As women's ministry leaders, our role may be simply sharing the publicity and encouraging sign-ups for churchwide service projects. As we'll discuss in more detail later, service projects can also be the focus of a women's ministry event or an easy add-on to an event we're already hosting.

Outreach is a reaching out into the community to bring people into the church. The focus is on extending an invitation to either a specific church event or weekly worship service. Examples of outreach include handing out flyers at a community event, holding a church event at a public location and inviting the community to attend, a fall festival, distributing Valentine's Day treats on a college campus, and so on. As women's ministry leaders, our role may be to encourage participation, share publicity, or to serve alongside the women in our church. While I hope all of your events are open to women outside of your church, your team may decide to host some events for the community with the goal of bringing in unchurched women.

Last, *evangelism* comes from the Greek word *euangelion*, which means "gospel" or "good news."[2] The *Holman Bible Dictionary* defines *evangelism* as the "active calling of people to respond to the message of grace and commit oneself to God in Jesus Christ."[3] While there may be opportunities to evangelize during a service project or outreach, that's not their primary intent. Missions are usually planned in such a way that evangelism *is* intentional and focused.

Everyone needs to hear the good news of the gospel! While you may determine that only specific events include a full gospel presentation, you should never miss the opportunity to share how women can receive Christ as their Lord and Savior. If the goal is for women to grow in their faith, they must first have faith. It can be tempting to assume that every woman in the room has heard the gospel and has responded to the gospel, but I've heard from enough women who were saved as adults to know that's not true. I hope and pray your women's ministry program includes regular opportunities for women to respond to the message of the gospel. Besides regularly sharing the gospel with the women attending your events and activities, I'd encourage you to train your women to share the gospel too. Your church may have a specific way of training your members, but there are also many evangelism methods you could use.

Never miss the opportunity to share how women can receive Christ as their Lord and Savior.

Nurturing Missions-Minded Women

Something incredibly beautiful happens when women answer God's call to serve. Relationships deepen, and shared experiences provide unbreakable points of connection. We move from being sisters in Christ sitting side by side at an event to being the hands of Jesus serving side by side in the community. We move from being a part of the church to being the church.

Service projects often appeal to women who may not attend the typical women's ministry events or fellowships. If you are struggling to reach younger women in your church, try adding opportunities to serve on and off campus. We broaden our reach and obey God's Word when service and missions become part of women's ministry.

Would you describe your women as missions-minded? Do they have a burning desire to share the gospel with those who are lost? Do they want to serve others? Do they see themselves as caregivers? Do they seek out opportunities to love those in need in your community? Do you see your women actively loving their neighbors?

While only God can transform sinful hearts into servant's hearts, there is much we can do to nurture that transformation.

While only God can transform sinful hearts into servant hearts, we can do much to nurture that transformation. We can provide regular opportunities for our women to serve others. Varying the types of service opportunities allows them to engage in missions at different levels—some they may find comfortable, and some that may stretch and grow them.

Let's look at four levels of mission participation:

1. **Prayer.** This is probably the easiest and perhaps the first step for many. As women pray for missionaries, mission trips, service projects, outreach events, and for the lost, their hearts begin to soften toward others in need.
2. **Donations.** Donating money or goods can be a launching point for future work with a ministry. When your team notices a need, it's easy to add a request for donations to the next women's ministry event. Examples include food drives for a local food pantry, toiletries for a local women's shelter, and bottled water for hurricane victims.

3. **One-time service projects.** One-and-done projects allow women to see the beginning and end of a project and may stoke interest in forming an ongoing relationship with the beneficiaries. Assembling back-to-school gifts for teachers is one example.
4. **Relationships.** When we enter into community with others, we can build godly relationships that extend far beyond prayers, donations, and one-time service projects. Partnering long-term with a local parachurch ministry can be fruitful for both those serving and those being served. Over time, your women may have opportunities to share the gospel and form discipling relationships.

We want to give our women multiple and different types of opportunities to serve others, encouraging them toward community and relationship. However, before we prayerfully seek out a new ministry partner or project, we need to have a clear understanding of what ministries and mission projects our church is already committed to and involved in. Remember, we want to complement, not compete.

Building Relationships with Parachurch Ministries

Where can your women join in where God is already at work? There are likely several parachurch ministries in your community that need regular volunteers. Again, start by checking with those your church already has a relationship with.

Several years ago, my women's ministry team helped to coordinate a food, cleaning supplies, and toiletries drive for a local women's shelter our church partnered with. (Yes, the same shelter I mentioned at the beginning of this chapter.) Little did we know how dropping off those supplies would change the direction of our women's ministry! Let me give you a little background first, so you can understand how God had already planted the seeds for this partnership.

A few months before the food drive, our team had rewritten our women's ministry mission statement. It read: "To glorify God through prayerfully planned activities and events for women in our church and community, which promote spiritual growth and lead women to Christ. We seek to serve women, both locally and internationally, with love and grace."

Through the process, God led us to a rather startling discovery: We weren't actively serving women locally or internationally. Like many other women's ministry teams, we were doing a great job of feeding the women in our church, but we neglected to look beyond our church walls and into the community. The answer wasn't to take an eraser to this new mission statement but to prayerfully seek ways to serve.

We began to ask God to show us what He would have us add to our ministry calendar. When we dropped off the food drive donations, one woman on our team casually asked the director if there were any other needs we could help with. A meeting followed, and the next thing I knew, we were bringing in lunch and providing an afternoon of pampering for the women at the shelter.

That was only the beginning of what God was going to do! We then made no-sew fleece blankets for them with plans to make more *with* them. We brainstormed ideas for game nights and craft nights. God didn't just light a fire for missions in our team members but other women in the church wanted to be a part of ministering to these women too. God surprised us all when the director at the shelter provided transportation so the women could come to the church for events. Several women even attended our trunk-or-treat event with their kids.

We never knew how long these precious ones would be at the women's shelter, but that did not matter. We embraced the opportunity God gave us to show them His love for however long we had a connection. God moved in the hearts of our women in a mighty way. He can do the same in your community.

Who Are the People in Your Neighborhood?

If you asked me, I might only know the names of about ten people on our street, even though there are more than forty houses. After nearly ten years of living in this neighborhood, I'm sad to say I haven't made more connections, despite Jesus's command in Matthew 22:37–39 to love my neighbors.

God has placed your women in neighborhoods filled with people who need Him and don't know Him. Perhaps God wants your women's ministry to equip and encourage your women to become local missionaries, serving and loving the people on their street. May we embrace the call to serve and love found in Galatians 5:13–14: "You, my brothers and sisters, were called to be free. But do not use your freedom to indulge the flesh; rather, serve one another humbly in love. For the entire law is fulfilled in keeping this one command: 'Love your neighbor as yourself.'"

Here are some questions to consider as you look for the women in your neighborhood:

1. **What about the communities in your church neighborhood?** Is there a school, apartment complex, trailer park, or fire station nearby where God is prompting you to build relationships? Rather than invite the women in the nearby apartment complex to come to the church for Bible study, what if you took Bible study to the apartment complex every week?

   Before you make excuses, pray and ask God to show you solutions. It's probably going to be messy and inconvenient, but the most worthwhile ministries are.

2. **Are there women who are already coming to the church building regularly but not staying?** Preschool moms. Basketball moms. Moms dropping their children off for VBS. Moms bringing a van full of middle schoolers to youth group. Invite those women to stay, rather than drop and run. Pray about whether God wants you to provide coffee and conversation or something more structured. One church leader recently reached out to me to share the fruit of their VBS outreach to women. Beautiful new friendships were formed, and women were shown the love of Christ.

3. **Is your church sharing space with another church?** One church my family attended provided meeting space for a Korean church. The sign in the front yard of the church was such a fixture that I rarely paid it much attention, but one day the Lord got my attention. Were we inviting these women to join us for our

women's Bible study and women's ministry events? A short discussion with the team and an email later, we made that very belated invitation. If language barriers are a concern, perhaps you're supposed to be part of the solution.

Ask God to open the eyes of your team to the mission field He wants your women to work in.

Just as my team overlooked the Korean church, it's easy to miss the mission fields you pass by regularly.

Creative Ideas for Adding Missions to Your Calendar

What are some practical and easy ways to add service activities and mission-oriented projects to your ministry calendar? Besides adding donation drives to a couple of women's ministry events each year, consider swapping out a craft activity for a service project. Instead of a holiday party for your women, host a holiday party for the residents at a nursing home and bring gifts for them rather than giving gifts to one another. You could add thirty minutes to the first Bible study session of the month to complete a service project together. Rather than hosting Bible study in your church building, what if you met in women's homes throughout your community and invited neighbors to attend? Search online for a list of Random Acts of Kindness (RAOK or RAK) and plan a night of RAOK in teams, meeting up for coffee and fellowship afterward. Don't just brainstorm with your team; ask your women where and how they'd like to serve. They may know needs that you aren't aware of, and they may even be willing to take the lead in coordinating the project. (Want more ideas? Check out the list of fifty-eight service project ideas in the resource section at the end of this chapter.)

A Few Words of Caution

I also want to offer a few words of caution. As authors Steve Corbett and Brian Fikkert state in the introduction of their book *When Helping Hurts: How to Alleviate Poverty Without Hurting the Poor . . . and Yourself*,

> When North American Christians do attempt to alleviate poverty, the methods used often do considerable harm to both the materially poor and the materially non-poor. Our concern is not just that these methods are wasting human, spiritual, financial, and organizational resources but that these methods are actually exacerbating the very problems they are trying to solve.[4]

Corbett and Fikkert advise,

> A first helpful step in thinking about working with the poor in any context is to discern whether the situation calls for relief, rehabilitation, or development. In fact, the failure to distinguish among these situations is one of the most common reasons that poverty-alleviation efforts often do harm.[5]

We have to take great care that our missions projects and activities help and don't harm those we work with. Will your donations take away income from a local store owner? Does your construction project prevent locals from working and earning a wage? Are you providing training that is needed and profitable? Is there a process in place to follow up or continue contact? Are your donations really wanted or needed? Research the parachurch ministries you are considering partnering with to make sure they have a plan in place not just for relief but for rehabilitation and development to help the people they are serving move from crisis to self-sufficiency.

As you prayerfully select a service or missions project, keep these things in mind:

- Take care that the way you collect donations allows for women in all financial positions to take part if they wish. No uncomfortable basket passing, please. Be grateful for donations of every size.
- Make sure your pastoral staff approves the project. Graciously accept their recommendations and direction.
- Open up the delivery of the donations to all of the women who came to the event (if possible). Your team should not be the only ones getting to take part in the blessing!

Be intentional with your missions projects. You and I want people to see Christ, not us.

The Challenge

What is God's desire for your women? Is He asking you to provide practical help and meet the physical needs of a ministry or community? Is He asking you to go into the community, love your neighbors, share the gospel, and build relationships? While one-and-done projects are worthwhile and much needed, you also need to make sure you involve your women in local missions work that builds relationships. Imagine the impact your women could make with their consistent presence and participation with just one ministry partner or neighborhood.

Reflection Questions

1. Make a list of the service and missions opportunities your team has offered in the last year. Label each with its level of participation (prayer, donations, one-time service projects, and relationships).

2. Create a list of parachurch ministries your team could prayerfully consider for a future partnership.

3. List at least three service project ideas you'd like your women to complete in the next year.

4. What did you find most encouraging or challenging in this chapter?

Praying Through the Process

Lord, we want to honor You by telling others about You. Please give our women boldness and confidence to share the gospel with those You place in their path. Help us develop servant hearts in our church through missions and service projects. Please show us who and where You want our women to serve. Amen.

Fifty-Eight Service Project Ideas

Craft, Cook, or Create

1. Take a meal to a widow, homebound member, single mom, or recent divorcée in your church.
2. Bake goodies, such as cupcakes, and deliver them to your local police or fire station.
3. Write letters or send cards to missionaries.
4. Gather to assemble no-sew fleece blankets for a local children's home or women's shelter.
5. Knit or crochet prayer shawls and lap blankets for church members and friends facing health challenges.
6. Sew some pillowcase dresses for children in another country.
7. Cut out shoes for Sole Hope.
8. Put together care kits and distribute them to those experiencing homelessness.
9. Host a sandwich-making party and pass them out to those experiencing homelessness.
10. Assemble and distribute blessing bags for women who need some encouragement.
11. Send college care packages.
12. Put together Sonshine boxes or bags and bless women in your church or community.
13. Fill a freezer with meals for a new mom.
14. Create birthday bags for your local food pantry (birthday cake mix, hats, candles, balloons).
15. Paint and decorate the teachers' lounge at a struggling school.
16. Create a community garden.
17. Decorate the bathrooms at a local school with positive messages.
18. Provide a meal for families at your local Ronald McDonald House.

Donate and Shop with a Purpose

19. Donate food to a local food pantry.
20. Gather and donate toiletries, makeup, and new underwear for a local women's shelter or sex trafficking ministry.
21. Bless a children's hospital with fun Band-Aids.
22. Purchase presents for a local Angel Tree.
23. Sponsor a family at a local school for Christmas.
24. Pack and distribute Thanksgiving baskets (turkey, stuffing, mashed potatoes, gravy, canned veggies, cranberry sauce) for families in need.
25. Collect gently used clothes and donate them to a ministry in need.
26. Hold a diaper drive for your local pregnancy ministry.
27. Donate children's books and movies to a local children's hospital.
28. Fill backpacks with school supplies for a teacher or school.
29. Hold a book drive for a local elementary school in need.
30. Host a baby shower for a local pregnancy center to help them restock supplies for pregnant and new mothers.
31. Hold a clothing drive for a local clothes closet ministry—or start your own!
32. Gather hats, scarves, and gloves for elementary school students in need.
33. Plan an Operation Christmas Child packing party for your neighborhood, church, or Bible study group.

Perform RAOK

34. Deliver bags of groceries, firewood, or gift cards to a local family in need.
35. Tape quarters or dollar bills to the vending machines in the waiting room of your local hospital.
36. Leave quarters and washing detergent at your local laundromat.
37. Pass out bottled water to construction workers on a hot day.
38. Distribute bottles of bubbles at the park for families to use.
39. Host a block party in a community near your church.
40. Purchase coloring books and crayons and leave them in hospital or urgent care waiting rooms.

Volunteer Your Time

41. Volunteer to clean and organize at your local food pantry.
42. Work a shift at a local soup kitchen.
43. Find a local field or farm that allows folks to glean.
44. Volunteer at a local women's shelter, homeless shelter, or another ministry in need.
45. Clean the home of an elderly person or homebound member of your church.
46. Take care of some yardwork or handyman chores for widows in your church.
47. Volunteer to help a refugee family complete paperwork, register for school, and so forth.
48. Adopt a classroom at a school with low student test scores.
49. Visit a nursing home and host a game of bingo.
50. Sing Christmas carols at a nursing home or children's hospital.
51. Cheer at a Special Olympics or special needs sporting event.
52. Take on a Meals on Wheels route.
53. Plan a Habitat for Humanity workday.
54. Organize a free car care clinic for single moms in your community.
55. Clean the roadside—consider adopting a highway near your church.
56. Add some beauty and fresh landscaping to a school.
57. Take sermon recordings to homebound church members.
58. Organize a blood drive.

**Please note: Inclusion on this list is not a blanket endorsement for any ministry that is specifically named.*

EIGHT

Communicating Clearly

Reaching the Women You Serve

May these words of my mouth and this meditation of my heart
be pleasing in your sight,
LORD, my Rock and my Redeemer.

Psalm 19:14

Have you ever ordered a specific dish off a menu because the description made your mouth water? I'm not a big fan of salmon, but when I came across the Korean glazed salmon (fresh chargrilled salmon topped with a Korean glaze served over a bed of creamy street corn and blistered asparagus) on the menu at one of our favorite restaurants at the beach, I didn't hesitate. I'm so glad I didn't—it was as good as it sounded!

Words have the power to influence our behavior. How we describe and publicize our events can have an impact on how quickly women sign up and whether or not they attend. If we don't use our words to communicate information about our events, women can't come.

Gone are the days when photocopied ministry newsletters and flyers in the bathroom stall were the best and often only necessary publicity for women's ministry events. Today we have multiple means of communicating information—email, text, social media, apps, newsletters, and more. How do we decide what's best?

In this chapter, we'll discuss the power of words and examine which channels of communication may be most effective for your women. I'll also share some tips for creating captivating publicity and using social media effectively.

Wisdom from the Word

The Bible has a lot to say about words. Words have power. Most importantly, *God's* words have power. In Genesis 1, God used His words to create the world. "God said, 'Let there be light,' and there was light" (v. 3). God spoke the sky, the land, the seas, and all living creatures into being. After God created humans in His image, He used His words to bless them and gave them instructions: "Be fruitful and increase in number; fill the earth and subdue it. Rule over the fish in the sea and the birds in the sky and over every living creature that moves on the ground" (v. 28). And God continues to communicate to us today through His Word, the Bible.

God has given us the ability to use words to communicate too. Our words may not wield the same power (we can't create something from nothing), but they can still have great impact. Our words have the power to build up and tear down (Eph. 4:29). Our words can offer forgiveness and cause destruction and division. Our words can share truth and mislead.

Ultimately, God wants us to use our words for good and for His glory. Our words should reflect His love, grace, and truth. With our words, we can encourage the women we serve. We can foster unity and community. We can use our words to pray for our women and share the gospel with them.

When my boys were young, there was a season in which they were especially careless with their words. One consequence of their carelessness was that they had to repeat Psalm 19:14 from memory before being released from time-out. It wasn't long before we all knew those words by heart: "May these words of my mouth and this meditation of my heart be pleasing in your sight, Lord, my Rock and my Redeemer." When we look at that verse in context, we see it comes at the end of a song by King David extolling the grandeur of God and His Word. David hopes that the words he has sung have pleased God. But it's not only those fourteen verses that David hopes please God; David wants God to be pleased with all the words that come out of his mouth. I hope the same for us. I hope our words will please God. It's my prayer that the words we use to communicate with our women and our team members will always glorify God. And when they don't, I pray we'll be quick to repent and seek forgiveness.

Ministry Memory

I've always loved words. I am a verbal processor, which means I use a lot of words before I get to the point. In elementary school I created my own classroom newspaper, and I recorded secret thoughts in my diary.

I've always felt one of my strengths is crafting words into publicity pieces for our women's ministry events. I love using my words to inspire women to take action. I have also learned the importance of utilizing every tool possible to get the word out about our women's ministry events. Announcements, bathroom fliers, Sunday bulletins, emails, and social media are all used to launch multipronged, coordinated publicity blitzes. Yet, despite these efforts, sometimes women in our church are unaware of our women's ministry plans.

I stood dumbfounded one day as a woman at my church complained to me that she hadn't heard about our most recent women's ministry event. How could she have missed the emails, social media posts, announcements in our small groups, and registration on the church website? While I wanted to be sympathetic, I was struggling to respond "full of grace" (Col. 4:6). I knew we had done a good job with our publicity. How did she not know? I couldn't think of anything more we could have done to get the word out, but it still wasn't enough.

Channels of Communication

How do your women prefer to receive communication from you? Is a text best? Do they check their email inboxes regularly? Are they on social media? If so, which platforms? Can you trust the algorithm to show them your posts? Will they read the notice in the Sunday bulletin or the slides before the start of the worship service? Are you trusting they'll search for the information they need on the church website or app?

While we'd like to think women will eagerly seek out information about the next women's ministry event, that rarely happens. It's up to us to get the information to them. Rather than posting on every social media app and plastering posters on every church wall, it is better to craft a strategy. Where are your women most likely to see the information you need to share? Where do they hang out in your church building? Where do they spend their time online?

While there are many places you can communicate, I recommend prioritizing these six options if they are available in your church:

1. Email
2. Text
3. Social media
4. Online registration form on your church's website
5. Announcements from the pulpit
6. Bulletin announcements and/or pre-worship slides

Additionally, you should be able to easily observe the traffic patterns of the women in your church and position publicity materials in their path. Yes, putting flyers in the bathroom still works! Just please make sure you get the proper approvals before displaying any new publicity in your church.

For one-time events such as a conference, Christmas dinner, or special speaker, you may want to deploy a broader publicity strategy. Here's a list of ten additional publicity ideas your team may want to use to get the word out:

1. Bulletin boards
2. Video announcements during service or on screens throughout your building
3. Bathroom flyers
4. Sunday school or small group announcements
5. Announcements at events and Bible studies
6. Save the date cards
7. Personal invitations
8. Postcards mailed or distributed before services

9. Banners
10. Registration tables

Most churches place a limit on announcements during the worship service. It can be very helpful to understand your church's communication guidelines and deadlines. Choose carefully which events need a bigger publicity push.

Emails and Texting

Even as the numbers of social media users rise, the most effective way to reach the majority of women is email and texting. Not everyone is on social media, so prioritizing emails and texts allows your team to contact virtually every woman in your church. Decide as a team what information will be distributed via text versus email and how often.

Many churches have invested in software programs that allow you to email or text a segment of church attendees. You may just need to ask if you can have access. If that isn't an option, you will need to build your own email list or text list. I do not recommend using a personal email account or setting up a group text thread, even if your church is small. There are several online services you can use for free with up to a certain number of subscribers. As of this writing, Mailchimp or Mailerlite may be good options for email, and Remind, SlickText, Reach, Flocknote, and Text in Church are some programs leaders use to text their women. Need help collecting those emails and cell numbers? Ask women at every function to fill out an information card, and include a place for them to opt-in to communication from your women's ministry team.

What are the benefits of using an email list or texting service?

1. **Access.** One of the most important benefits of using a service is shared access with women's ministry team members. If only one person has all the email addresses or cell numbers, the rest of the team must rely on that person's availability and ability to send out information correctly and promptly.
2. **Ease.** You can easily add new women to the email list or texting service.

3. **Replies.** You eliminate the ability of your women to "reply all." This prevents them from intentionally or unintentionally sending spam or personal information to the entire group.
4. **Privacy.** Your women's ministry email addresses and cell numbers are stored securely and are not available for everyone on the text or email to see.
5. **Email delivery.** Not sure if your women received your email? Now you can check. Most services provide detailed reports that allow you to see who opened each email and who did not. You may even wish to resend your email to those who didn't open it the first time.
6. **Email templates.** Most email list services allow you to create templates so all of your emails have a similar look and style. Links to social media and your website can be embedded at the bottom of each email too. There's no need to create a pretty PDF or send plain text—you can customize your emails, and they'll look professional and impressive!

While not all of your women may be active on social media, almost all of them have an email address and/or cell phone number. Using email and texts in addition to printed publicity materials increases the likelihood that your women will see the information you've sent out.

Women's Ministry Newsletters

Many women's ministry teams find it helpful to create a quarterly or monthly ministry newsletter. While most of the women in your church are probably active email users, you may find that some of your older women do not have an email account and some of your younger women may not regularly check their email inbox. To make sure your newsletter is available to every woman in your church, you may want to provide printed copies in addition to sending it via email. When newsletters are sent out regularly, recipients begin to expect and look for them, making them a very effective publicity tool.

What should you include in a women's ministry newsletter? While there are many options, here are some things you may want in every issue:

1. The message of salvation. Women need to know how they can become a follower of Christ. Your pastor should be able to point you to some resources if you need help writing it out.
2. Contact information for your women's ministry, including links to social media accounts and an email address.
3. A list of your team members, with roles noted.
4. Calendar of upcoming events so they can save the date.
5. A past event summary—let them know what they've been missing!
6. Mission needs, including any donation collections or service opportunities.
7. Detailed upcoming event information.

You may also want to include these items:

1. An interview or devotional.
2. An encouraging verse.
3. The theme and Scripture verse for the year.
4. A recipe from a recent event.

Please check the copyright information for anything you're sharing from a book, magazine, website, blog post, or other previously published resource. In most cases, you'll need to receive written permission from the author to share it. Be sure to properly cite the source too.

What do other leaders include in their women's ministry newsletter? A women's ministry leader I know at a small neighborhood church in Indianapolis sends out a quarterly newsletter that includes upcoming birthdays, prayer requests, a member highlight, events information, a devotional, and a member's favorite recipe. A women's ministry director for a multicampus church in Virginia has found that her newsletters need to be short and easily read on a phone screen. She sends out a monthly newsletter that includes a brief devotional, a prayer, a list of upcoming event dates, a spotlight (information about a leader, volunteer, mentor, or mentee), and instructions on how to find a small group. Other leaders have mentioned including a list of recommended resources (books and podcasts), prayer concerns, Scripture reading lists, memory verse challenges, and information about church-supported missionaries.

Women's ministry newsletters are more than just another publicity tool. Newsletters can:

- Encourage women in their spiritual walk.
- Serve as an introduction to women's ministry in welcome packets for church guests.
- Provide an opportunity for women with the gift of writing to serve in your women's ministry.

The most effective women's ministry newsletters are created with a clear purpose in mind and are sent out consistently. The idea lists above are lengthy, but there's nothing wrong with a short and sweet newsletter that communicates only the most important information your women need so they can participate in your next women's ministry events and activities.

Social Media

You or your team members may dread the thought of using social media for your women's ministry. I understand. Social media can be the source of a lot of drama and negativity. You may even debate the wisdom of asking women to spend more time on their devices. Think of it instead as taking the message to a space where many of your women already are. Unlike email, women can interact with the information you post on social media. They might ask a question, express their excitement for your upcoming event, or use the "share" button to invite others to attend.

With so many different options available and new platforms popping up regularly, you may be unsure about where to start. How can your team determine which social media channel(s) will be most effective for your ministry? The quickest and easiest way is to ask your women which ones they use regularly. This is one of those times where the majority should rule. Let your numbers determine your focus, and go where most of your women already spend their time. Because social media usage usually varies by age, you may need to use two different social media channels to reach all of your women effectively. At the time of this writing, Facebook is a better target for those over forty, and Instagram will be more likely to reach those under forty.

Algorithms, the mystical formula social media companies use to display and rank the items in your social media feed, are constantly changing. If you have a woman on your team who understands the best practices for posting on social media, regularly seek her advice. Not everyone who follows your Instagram account or is a member of your Facebook group will see every single thing you post. You might post five times about an event, but Keisha may only see two of those posts. Share more than you think you need to! Ask your team members to like, comment, and share your online content to help extend its visibility and reach.

Most ministry teams find it helpful to have a private space where prayer requests and conversations can't be viewed by those outside of the group. Your church may have an app or program they would prefer you use. If not, free apps such as GroupMe, Slack, WhatsApp, or Signal are some ways leaders communicate with their women between physical meetings. Some teams prefer using an app because it allows women who are not on social media to participate. These apps can be a powerful tool for building community, but they require commitment and oversight. Your group will need admins to post information, approve new group members, monitor the conversation, and delete any posts that fail to stay within group guidelines.

What about Facebook pages and groups? Pages talk to your audience, while groups encourage conversation with your audience. If you're going to use social media, I recommend setting up a private Facebook group rather than a Facebook page for your women's ministry. Groups provide a level of community and confidentiality your women will appreciate.

You may be surprised by the connections that can occur inside a private Facebook group or an app. One leader shared with me the snowball effect that a simple icebreaker question had inside their Facebook group. Their social media manager posted a question, asking, "What is your favorite restaurant for eating lunch?" The recommendations poured in, and then women started making plans in the comments to meet each other for lunch!

To keep your social media account from becoming a source of division or distraction, your team will need to set some guidelines.

How to avoid social media pitfalls:

1. **Determine the purpose of your social media account and put it in writing.** Share the purpose in your account's description so new members understand your focus.
2. **Create posting and group guidelines.** What should be posted? What types of posts won't be permitted? Being proactive and not reactive will benefit everyone. Take into consideration political posts; self-promotion; videos, quotes, or articles that may differ theologically from your church's beliefs; prayer requests; complaints; and so forth. Outline a plan for dealing with posting violations.
3. **Recruit someone to serve as your social media manager.** They should also serve as a member of the women's ministry leadership team. Having someone committed to overseeing and scheduling your social media posts will provide the consistency needed to encourage engagement. This person should also address violations to your posting guidelines immediately and consistently.

Lack of engagement is one frustration that leaders often encounter in setting up a social media account. Prime the pump by asking your women's ministry team members to comment on and like the posts. Sometimes women are waiting for someone else to go first. Your team is also modeling the activity that you desire. Respond to comments as you are able. While your social media manager may not respond to every single comment, it takes mere moments to hit the "like" button. The more you interact with and respond to comments, the more your women will comment and reply. Creating an active online community takes time. Expect interaction to ebb and flow.

While our primary purpose includes encouraging women to grow in their love and knowledge of God, we also want them to grow in their relationships with each other. Posts that encourage women to share will help strengthen those connections. Here are some social media post ideas:

- **Bible verse graphics.** Consider sharing the context of the verse.
- **Prayer prompts.** Invite your women to join your team in praying for specific groups of people, missionaries, or topics.

- **Ministry updates.** Share testimonials from a recent event or activity. Encourage retreat registration by announcing the shrinking number of remaining tickets, for example.
- **Event publicity.** Share event information, including registration deadlines, speaker photos, registration links, donation collections, sneak peek photos, teasers, and childcare sign-up.
- **Feedback requests.** The polling features on social media can provide instant feedback to help your team make decisions and plans. Use polls just for fun too! Examples: Do you prefer coffee or tea? Beach or mountains?
- **Short teachings or personal stories.** Consider asking specific women in your church to write or record a short teaching or story. Reach out to women in your church who are Bible study teachers, speakers, and authors; they may be willing to help.
- **Links to biblically sound resources.** Check with your church staff for a list of recommended podcasts, apps, pastors, authors, and websites.
- **Photos.** Share images from past events and for upcoming events.
- **Videos.** Share highlights from a past event, create a promo video for an upcoming event, record and share testimonies, or interview team members or women in your church.
- **Icebreaker questions.** Consider using a mix of fun and faith-focused questions. Icebreakers encourage interaction and provide connection opportunities.
- **Music playlists.** Create and share a song list for your event or share the worship songs from Sunday's service.
- **Inspirational quotes.** Make certain any quote you share from someone, living or dead, lines up with the beliefs of your church. To avoid any issues that might arise if an author, speaker, or pastor changes their theological position, you may wish to quote only trusted, famous Christian people who have died.

Using a social media schedule will keep your social media manager and your women from being overwhelmed. I suggest creating a weekly plan with three or four posts per week. Consistency will also encourage engagement. Decide what type of post (from those listed above) you want to create or share each day of the week. Here's a sample schedule to get your wheels turning:

Sunday: A Bible verse.

Monday: A fun icebreaker question or publicity for an upcoming event.

Wednesday: Prayer requests and praises.

Friday: A faith-focused icebreaker question.

Having a written weekly schedule will simplify the process and minimize the time needed to schedule posts and help you keep the focus on Christ. You can always change up the types of posts to communicate important event information or point women toward time-sensitive resources.

Learning how to use technology can be time-consuming and even frustrating at times, but it's worth the work to nurture relationships when not meeting together in person. Relationships are more likely to flourish if there's consistent communication and interaction. Social media can fill the need for a connection between ministry meetings. You may even find that your attendance increases as women look forward to connecting in person.

Church Websites and Apps

Church websites and apps are a great place for guests to discover information about your women's ministry program. It's helpful to have a dedicated women's ministry page. On that page, you may want to include:

1. Contact information (name and email address for your women's ministry director)
2. Links to social media accounts
3. Mission statement
4. Brief explanation of what women can expect (types of events and frequency)

5. Photos of women in your church at an event
6. Link to a registration page for upcoming events
7. Links to other applicable pages, such as women's Bible study or small groups

You may not have access to make regular updates to this page, so try to keep the content evergreen (always applicable). Outdated ministry information might lead women to think your women's ministry is no longer active.

What to Include in Your Publicity Materials

I can't tell you how many times I've failed to include a key piece of information in my publicity materials. I also distinctly remember opening up my Sunday morning bulletin one day to discover that it listed the wrong start time for an event our women's ministry team was hosting. When I followed up with the team member in charge of publicity, she thought it was accurate. In the grand scheme of things, it really wasn't a big deal, as the event time was only off by half an hour, but it highlighted the need to communicate details more effectively among team members and necessitated some tweaks to the event agenda. It is best to always follow up in writing with the key details of your event for your team members to avoid this kind of confusion.

And speaking of confusion, will guests or new members in your church have all the information they need? My current church has a "fireside room," and it took me months to figure out where that space was. It was only referred to by name and never by location. This list will help ensure you share those details that we sometimes assume everyone knows:

- Name of the event*
- Location*
- Time*
- Date*
- Day of the week
- Cost*
- Childcare (cost, registration info, or not available)

- Registration information (if needed)
- A brief description of the event*
- Ministry logo
- Contact information (website, church office, or email)*
- What participants need to bring (Bible, donations, craft supplies, love offering)

**These items should be included in shorter publicity pieces where space is limited, with directions on how to find out more information. I've included a publicity form in the resource section at the end of this chapter to help you communicate with clarity and consistency.*

How to Create Captivating Publicity Materials

Outdated publicity materials can be a real turnoff for the younger women in your church. They subliminally send the message that your women's ministry team doesn't prioritize publicity or that your ministry is primarily for older women.

If you are blessed to have a women's ministry team member or staff member who can create publicity materials and graphics for you, stop and take a moment to send them a thank-you note. Most women's ministry leaders are not so fortunate. Even if not, you can still create captivating publicity materials; it's just going to take a little effort.

Before selecting the DIY route, search among your women for someone with graphic design experience who can help. If that search isn't fruitful, thankfully there are many apps and websites that provide templates you can easily tweak to match your event theme and decor (Canva is my go-to). Use the "resize" option to craft the social media graphics and printed materials you need so they all have a similar look and style.

It can be challenging to find Christian-themed free stock photos. If you can take your own photos, do it! In case you aren't aware, it is illegal to copy and paste images you find on the internet without obtaining permission. Yes, copyright lawyers really will send you a strongly worded, scary-sounding letter and threaten to take legal action. You must either take your own photos, purchase images, or find free stock images. Be sure to list the source if required. Don't forget to read the fine print and licensing info; that will tell you how you can and cannot use the image. For example, you might not be able to put an image on a T-shirt to sell at an event, but it may be okay for you to use it on a social media graphic. (Sidenote: If you're going to use a close-up photo of your women for publicity, please obtain their permission first. They'll also greatly appreciate it if you avoid using any awkward or unflattering photos.)

Quick tips for creating captivating publicity graphics:

1. Save the file as a PNG file for clearer images and fonts.
2. Select fonts, letter sizes, and colors that are easily readable.
3. Choose no more than three fonts for any project.
4. Have someone else double-check your spelling, details, and layout.

If this is outside of your comfort zone, don't panic! Most apps and websites offer tutorials to help you learn how to use their tools. You can also find many helpful videos on YouTube. It's worth pushing yourself over the learning curve.

Videos are the perfect vehicle for telling a story, and they show and tell women why they should attend. After years at the same retreat venue, our women will stay in a new place this year. A few of us were able to visit the new-to-us retreat center over the summer. While we were there, we took photos and videos of the things we can't wait for our women to experience. Change can be a bit unsettling. We wanted to create excitement about some of the new things they would experience. Consider sharing a behind-the-scenes sneak peek of your event, ask your speaker to introduce herself in a short video, or show off the amazing amenities at your retreat center. Keep the camera rolling at the event and record clips and testimonies to use in next year's publicity pieces.

Video tips:

- Use a microphone if available, and film in a quiet place.
- Use a flattering angle. Placing the camera slightly above the eyes, barely angled down, eliminates those up-the-nose shots.
- Stand near a window and add lighting if needed.

- Edit your footage.
- Add subtitles.
- Background music can add a nice touch, if it's not too loud.

Taking the time to create stylish publicity materials and videos will pay off.

How Often and How Soon?

The key to effective communication is clarity and consistency. If you're going to send out a monthly email newsletter, then be sure you send it out every month. If you're going to send a text two weeks before your event, then make a note on your calendar or schedule it in advance so you don't forget. Women need to see the information for your event or activity multiple times.

There's a classic marketing "rule of seven" that stated prospective customers would need to come across an offer at least seven times before they noticed it and started to take action. That's no longer the case—it's now more! Marketing expert Kathi Kruse notes, "today you might need more than those 7 times just to be heard above all the clutter that's in people's newsfeeds or fields of vision."[1] We want to present our information early and often.

How early is too early? That depends. For a higher priced or multiday event, you'll want women to know at least three to six months in advance. For our ministry's annual fall retreat, women are told to save the date one year in advance. We trickle the publicity about four months out. When we open registration three months before the event, we really ramp up our publicity efforts. For smaller-scale events, we typically focus our publicity efforts on the four weeks leading up to the close of registration or the event itself.

It's a multipronged effort each time. Here's what this can look like for our women's ministry team:

- An event is created in our private Facebook group.
- Graphics and registration links are posted on social media about once per week, sometimes more.

- Slides are shown before the church service, and if it's a big event, announcements are made from the stage.
- Our monthly newsletter is sent and includes event information.
- Often, but not always, one text is sent out to all the women of the church.
- Our church's communications team may publicize the event on social media and in the monthly pastor's video (though not all events receive that level of publicity).

Our team is great about sharing the information within their small groups and checking with friends to see if they've signed up. If we're struggling with sign-ups, we'll brainstorm at our team meeting or via text to think of some additional ways to get the word out. We've found a short video from our women's ministry director or the woman slated to teach at the event is helpful too.

As your team decides how often and how much publicity is best in your specific church, please remember to check with your church's communications team. They may have a publicity schedule for you to follow for churchwide publicity efforts.

Personal Invitations

Personal invites trump traditional publicity methods every single time. Several years ago, the women's ministry team I was serving on received some rather frustrating feedback on a survey. One woman mentioned that she had never attended a women's ministry event because nobody had ever invited her. Really? Though we disagreed with her comment, our team became more intentional about making personal invites to our activities and events. We also started including the words "You are invited" in publicity pieces.

There's something about knowing that your presence is desired that will move women to action. If you're part of a smaller church, issuing personal invitations may be time-consuming but manageable. But what if you're part of a larger church? How can you possibly personally invite every woman to attend? It can be done! For example, one team issues invitations through their small groups by asking one woman in each small group if she will serve as a women's ministry representative. She is provided the publicity information for every women's ministry event and then invites the women in her small group to attend. She might issue verbal invites and can also email, text, or post the details provided to her small group members.

Another church found a way to extend personal invitations to the women in their church who don't regularly attend women's ministry events. First, their team enlisted ten ladies to be table hostesses for their upcoming event. These hostesses were then asked to call and invite new people or people who may not be connected well to sit at their table. This spread out the work of making personal invitations and expanded the reach beyond the women serving on the women's ministry team.

Twelve Ways to Publicize Events to the Community

Not every event necessitates publicity outside of our church community, but when it comes to reaching those beyond our church walls, we sometimes struggle with how to get the word out. Here are a few ideas to add to your publicity arsenal:

1. Hang posters and tear-off flyers on community boards at the grocery store, coffee shop, and so forth.
2. Distribute flyers or invitation cards through your church's school or preschool.
3. Send Facebook invites to friends, neighbors, and family outside of your church.
4. Place large outdoor banners on the church property near the road for drivers to see.
5. Mail postcards to women in your church's zip code.
6. Set up a booth at a local fair (distribute water, provide a nursing station for moms).
7. Record a radio ad. Your local Christian station may air an ad or announcement for free.
8. Invest in Facebook ads (if your budget allows).

9. Place an ad in local community magazines and newspapers.
10. Request a TV interview (local morning or midday show).
11. Submit an article to neighborhood newsletters, apps, or websites.
12. Contact past attendees and invite them back (especially for similar or recurring events).

Women inside of and outside of our church cannot come if they do not know. As technology changes, we'll need to continue to adapt our publicity methods. The time, energy, and effort to reach more women for Christ is worth it!

Team Communication

How well does your team communicate between team meetings? What method do you use to share time-sensitive information and discuss urgent situations? The team I currently serve on moved away from group texts to a free messaging app a couple of years ago. For longer messages and attachments, we typically use email. On a few rare occasions, we've used Zoom or Facetime to include an out-of-town team member for an important meeting.

While there may be a few life updates and answers to prayer requests shared, remember to focus on women's ministry. Just as we discussed the importance of communicating often, accurately, and gracefully with your women, the same pertains to your leadership team. While it's fun to send funny memes, save those for one-on-one convos, not your team thread. When your team members know when and how you'll be sending out the meeting agenda and meeting minutes, they'll look for and expect them.

Reflection Questions

1. What publicity ideas does your team need to add to your publicity plan?

2. Which social media platforms do the women in your church use regularly?

3. Which social media platforms does your women's ministry use? Are they the same platforms your women use regularly (see above)?

4. Which technology tools do you sense God wants your team to use to nurture connection and increase communication?

5. What did you find most encouraging or challenging in this chapter?

Praying Through the Process

Lord, please help us be effective communicators. Help us spread the word about our activities and events. Help us create publicity that is appealing and accurate. Help us use technology as a tool to bring more women to You. Amen.

PUBLICITY FORM

Event Name:

Event Date:	Event Day:	Event Time (start and end):
Cost:	Location:	

Registration Information (how and when):

Childcare Information (if applicable):

Publicity Strategy:

- ☐ Email
- ☐ Text
- ☐ Social Media
- ☐ Sunday Morning Slide Deck
- ☐ Bathroom Stalls/Bulletin Boards
- ☐ Sunday Bulletin or Bulletin Insert
- ☐ Church Newsletter or Email Blast
- ☐ Church Website
- ☐ Other ____________________

Graphic(s) Needed:

Date to Begin Publicity:

Main Text for Publicity:

Twenty-Five Questions to Post on Social Media

1. What are you having for supper tonight?
2. What restaurant in town is your favorite place to eat lunch?
3. What is your favorite podcast?
4. What book are you currently reading or have read lately?
5. Describe your past week as a weather forecast.
6. What's something you said you'd never do, but you have?
7. If you could have an unlimited supply of one thing for the rest of your life, what would it be?
8. Name one ingredient that will always ruin the dish.
9. I've seen every episode of __________.
10. What's one book (besides the Bible) you think everyone should read?
11. Share a random line from a movie that fans will instantly know.
12. You have thirty minutes to spend $10,000 inside one store; where are you going?
13. What is something that should be taught in school but isn't?
14. What's the best animated movie?
15. People would say I use too many __________.
16. What is one book of the Bible you'd like to learn more about?
17. What is something you are praying for this week?
18. What is one thing you've learned from your time in God's Word this week?
19. What is one thing you enjoy about our church?
20. What is one thing you wish every person knew about God?
21. Share a tip for finding time to study God's Word.
22. Who is one woman in the Bible you'd like to learn more about?
23. What is one thing you learned from this week's sermon?
24. What's one thing you want people to know about Jesus?
25. What are you thankful for today?

NINE

Navigating Change and Addressing Sacred Cows

> Forget the former things;
>   do not dwell on the past.
> See, I am doing a new thing!
>   Now it springs up; do you not perceive it?
> I am making a way in the wilderness
>   and streams in the wasteland.
>
> Isaiah 43:18–19

Chances are, in the previous pages you've come across some ideas that will require a change in the way you currently administer the women's ministry program in your church. You may be excited about the potential results of making those changes but are unsure of how best to approach them. Your women's ministry team members may need some time to process and pray. You know these changes are likely to ruffle a few feathers, and you fear you'll encounter some severe backlash. You may wonder, *Should I even bother? Do I want to battle any opposition? Will it be worth it?* I've wondered those very same things.

In this chapter, we'll talk about the sacred cows in women's ministry. We'll look at ways to assess ministry events and activities to determine when and where God may be leading your team to make some changes. I'll also share some tips for dealing with opposition. Change is often uncomfortable and requires overcoming resistance. While you may not be able to win over every woman in your church, you can smooth the transitions.

Wisdom from the Word

As I was thinking about times in which God's people have confronted situations that required them to change, one particular passage stood out: the recon mission of the twelve spies into the promised land. Moses knew the Israelites would have lots of questions about this new land, so he gave the spies a list of questions to answer. "See what the land is like and whether the people who live there are strong or weak, few or many. What kind of land do they live in? Is it good or bad? What kind of towns do they live in? Are they unwalled or fortified? How is the soil? Is it fertile or poor? Are there trees in it or not?" (Num. 13:18–20). They were also told to bring back a sample of any fruit they found.

The spies spent forty days exploring the promised land and seeking answers to these questions. Grapes, pomegranates, and figs were gathered and carried home. Their report, in the beginning, looked quite promising. The land was rich, overflowing with fruit, milk, and honey. Some expressed concerns because "the people who live there are powerful, and the cities are fortified and very large" (v. 28). Caleb, however, was confident they should proceed to the promised land, just as the Lord had said. Ten of the spies weren't so easily convinced and had serious doubts: "We can't attack those people; they are stronger than we are" (v. 31). It wasn't just that they were stronger; they were larger too! So much so that the spies seemed like grasshoppers. Fear overtook the Israelites, and that night they wept out loud (14:1). They couldn't imagine moving forward with the Lord's plans and suggested it would be better to pick a new leader and go back to Egypt, where they were slaves. Joshua spoke up and urged the people not to fall prey to their fears but to move forward and obey the plans of the Lord. The Israelites responded by threatening to stone him.

The Israelites trusted in themselves and not the Lord. As a result, an entire generation, except for Joshua and Caleb, died before entering the promised land. Fear of an unknown future caused an entire generation to miss out on God's blessings.

Ministry Memory

I can relate to the fear of making changes and going in a new direction. Many years ago, during one of my check-in meetings with the pastor overseeing our women's ministry program, we had an honest, off-the-record chat about making a change to our most popular women's ministry event, the big table event I mentioned in chapter 5. This annual event was no longer serving its original purpose. The attendance was fantastic, but the focus was lacking. Instead of gathering a large number of women for dinner, biblical teaching, and encouragement, the decorations had become the focal point. Hours upon hours were spent decorating each table and the stage where the speaker stood. While the decorations team was incredibly gifted and the result was beautiful, the sheer amount of decorations was a distraction. Decor trumped content, and there was little focus on the gospel.

The pastor and I talked through several options, including cancelling the event. While I was sorely tempted, I knew the backlash would be brutal, even with his backing. I believed we could make the event better and still keep our women happy. We decided to make several small changes that year, with plans to make more over time. Moving slowly meant we didn't leave our women behind. The gradual shift brought the event back in line with our purpose without the risk of alienating a large number of participants.

Is It Time to Kill a Sacred Cow?

Years later, when I came across the phrase "sacred cow," I knew without question that is what this table event had become. Robert Kriegel and David Brandt, in their book *Sacred Cows Make the Best Burgers*, define sacred cows as "an outmoded belief, assumption, practice, policy, system or strategy, generally invisible, that inhibits change and prevents responsiveness to new opportunities."[1] While Kriegel and Brandt are speaking in terms of businesses, it's not a stretch to see how this principle applies in the local church as well. You can probably think of a practice or policy in your church that is outdated and in need of some change. Maybe it's the way the Christmas decorations are displayed or the process by which your retreat speaker is selected.

Author Thom S. Rainer can help us with church-specific applications of this idea of sacred cows. Rainer describes sacred cows as a term "commonly used in churches to describe those facets of church life that are given undue (and sometimes unbiblical) respect to the point they cannot be changed."[2]

Common sacred cows in women's ministry include:

- Annual table events
- Secret sisters
- Retreat locations
- Unspoken dress codes
- Event schedules
- Holiday parties
- Long-held traditions

It can sometimes be difficult for longtime church members to identify sacred cows, as they may be so ingrained in the church culture. New church members are often unaware of sacred cows until they innocently suggest their removal.

A few years ago, I stumbled upon a sacred cow in our women's Bible study program. I made a suggestion to pivot from using two larger rooms to a couple of smaller, more private Sunday school rooms for the discussion group portion of our time together. The rest of the team members were confused because there wasn't room to set up tables in those spaces. I didn't immediately understand why that was a problem, as I had spent years attending a community Bible study program where we had always sat in a circle of chairs and held our materials on our laps.

I didn't know that the women in this church *always* sat at tables for Bible study. Be warned: Just because you don't view something as a sacred cow doesn't mean your ladies don't!

One of our group facilitators insisted her group continue to use a room with tables, and the other agreed to try a room without tables but was skeptical it would work. It did work, but for many of our women it was a bit of an adjustment. It took them time to appreciate the privacy and lack of disruption that were offered by using those smaller rooms instead.

Sometimes the need for change is obvious, and sometimes it isn't. Here are some signs it's time for a change:

- Attendance has fallen for this event or activity, either as a whole or by age group.
- The event follows the same schedule (maybe even the same speaker) year after year after year.
- The enthusiasm for this event has waned.
- The focus of the event is on something other than Jesus and God's Word.
- The event or activity no longer aligns with your women's ministry mission statement or the church's mission.
- The event fails to draw in new women from inside or outside the church.
- The same woman continues to coordinate the event year after year.

Eliminating a tradition, especially one that has become what some might call a sacred cow, can cause serious division. This, unfortunately, is something I have experience with.

Before Making a Change or Killing a Sacred Cow

If you feel it's time to bring an end to a beloved women's ministry tradition, or you sense God's leading to kill a sacred cow, spend time in prayer over this decision before doing anything. You must be confident that the Lord is bringing this event or activity to an end. Write down why you feel this is the direction the team should go, so you are prepared to articulate your decision.

Don't be a lone ranger. Changes need to be a team decision, or your ministry could be negatively affected. If you feel confident an event or activity does not serve the purposes of your women's ministry, take the time to help your team reach that same conclusion. Kriegel and Brandt advise leaders to offer respect, understanding, and acknowledgment to build loyalty among your team, which will help propel you through the process of change.[3] In other words, "Ownership will make them work harder to make change work."[4]

Again, it's important to speak with your supervising pastor. You want their input and their backing. Women who disagree with the change your team has made might take their complaints straight to the top. Some pastors may even use their authority to press pause on the event, which removes some of the blame from you and your team.

Once your team and pastor are on board, it's time to share that vision with other women. Reach out to those with the greatest influence and spend time addressing any of their concerns. You may find they are excited about the new direction in which God is leading!

Are You Operating in a Silo?

I don't recall the first time I was exposed to the concept of silo ministries, but the accusation that women's ministry operates in a silo was one that hit a little too close to home. A silo ministry is just as it sounds: it operates on its own without oversight or input from others. In Romans 12:4, Paul combats such individualistic thinking by reminding his audience that they are "one body with many members, and these members do not all have the same function." We need to operate as one body—the church body—not a separate entity.

It can be easy for a women's ministry to operate in a silo, especially if it is led by a lay leader and not a paid staff member. Your women's ministry director may not be included in church staff meetings or planning sessions. Regardless, take strides to ensure your ministry plans complement and don't compete with other ministry plans in the church. Those regular meetings with your overseeing pastor I mentioned earlier can prevent silo operations. If there's even a hint that your ministry is operating in a silo, that may be a sign it's time to make some changes.

Evaluations Can Encourage Change

Change that comes from a team decision instead of a single person is often better received. You're able to skip the step of getting your team on board with the idea. Constant evaluation of events and activities will lead your team to identify areas where change would be beneficial. Have your team complete a post-event evaluation form (shared in chapter 5) after each event. You can also annually assess your women's ministry program using a ministry health assessment (see the resource section at the end of this chapter).

When you sit down to work on your schedule for the year (or half year), examine every event or activity before it is placed on the calendar.

Ask your team these three questions:

1. Does it need to be refined?
2. Should it be removed?
3. Is it something that should remain?

But how do you decide if it should remain, be removed, or be refined? Once you've begun filling out post-event evaluation forms for each event, you'll likely have a good handle on answering those questions. Please know I am not recommending you go back and fill one out for every event or activity you have completed in the past year! That's way too much work. Instead, ask your team some of these questions:

- Does this event meet a need?
- Does it encourage spiritual growth?
- Does it allow opportunities for outreach and service?
- Are we sharing the gospel?
- Is it open to visitors and the community?
- Is it relevant, or has it become outdated?
- Are we reaching multiple age groups?
- Does it need refreshing or repackaging?
- Should it be shelved for a year or two so that something new can be tried?
- Is our calendar too full?

Admittedly, removing an event sounds like something to be avoided at all costs, but it doesn't have to be. It is better to remove a popular program while it's still popular rather than waiting until it isn't. Focus on ending on a high note rather than risk losing women over time. When removing an activity or event, be sure to have a replacement ready—unless your calendar is too crowded.

God may lead you to refine your event instead of remove it. It's also possible that reworking the event or activity could prevent the need to permanently remove it. That annual table event I've mentioned was identified as a sacred cow, but pulling the plug abruptly on this beloved event would likely have resulted in a revolt, so the team implemented two changes the next year to direct the focus from the decor to the message.

God may lead you to refine your event instead of remove it.

Our second change, as I mentioned in the chapter on mentoring and discipleship, was to include a speaker who would draw in our younger women. Attendance in years past was significantly skewed to an older crowd, which led most of our younger women to believe this event was not for them. Our youngest speaker that night was well-known and much-loved by the younger women in our church. Her friends were excited to show up to hear her speak. Success!

If God is leading you down the path of refining, you can:

- Seek input from across the generations.
- Update when possible (fresh graphics, new theme, new technology, and so on).
- Add a service or outreach component.
- Change the program order (for example, start with the speaker and end with dinner).
- Change the day, time, schedule, length, or location.
- Add depth.
- Remove anything unnecessary.
- Keep the meat (don't skimp on the message).

Before axing an event, try making a change. Change the schedule, change the location, or change the emphasis, but don't change *everything* at once. Make incremental changes over several years until the event becomes what you feel God is leading it to be. Or consider hosting the event in alternating years. This can be especially beneficial if the event or activity is a drain on the women's ministry budget. When women see what else can be done with those funds, they might not hold on so tightly to that event. Make every tweak, adjustment, or change a matter of prayer. God's timing and His will for your church and your women are most important. We may be ready for change, but it may not yet be God's timing.

How Not to Kill a Sacred Cow

Many years ago, I tried to bring an abrupt end to a program called Secret Sisters at a church in which I served. I admit, I wasn't a big fan of Secret Sisters. It was designed to connect women in the church through the secret giving of cards and gifts for an entire year. At the end of the year, a brunch was held to reveal who your secret sister was. In our church, participation was low (about twenty-five women out of five hundred). Though it was open to all our women, every participant was sixty or older.

I had many concerns:

- The purpose was lacking a focus on Christ.
- The budget for the reveal brunch was bigger than all our other women's ministry events.
- Women could only join once a year, which excluded anyone new from participating.
- Some registrants failed to participate, which meant one could show love to a secret sister but receive nothing in return. The risk of hurt feelings was high.
- Our younger women were not interested in the program.
- It was inward focused, rather than outward focused.

It's been many years, so some of the details are fuzzy, but as I recall, I didn't do enough to address my concerns before omitting the program from the budget proposal. I failed to follow the previously mentioned steps and suffered the consequences.

When I explained my concerns to the team, emphasizing that I did not feel spending that much money on an event that only about twenty-five women participated in was in line with the rest of our budget, a couple of team members were quick to find ways to cut the cost of the reveal party. In the end, they decided to charge each woman $10 for the brunch that year, and it was decided I would draft a letter (to be reviewed and approved by our pastor) to all the participants letting them know we would suspend the Secret Sisters program for the following year. It was a difficult meeting, and I left feeling like I had made some enemies that day. The brunch went on as planned, minus the high price tag, and we pressed pause on Secret Sisters for the next year. It was the right decision, but I went about it all wrong. I pray you won't do the same!

Hold the Line

While my approach to removing the sacred cow of Secret Sisters was lacking, my reasons for removing that activity were spot-on. Secret Sisters failed to meet the requirements in our mission statement. As you determine what remains, what's removed, and what's refined in your ministry, your mission statement can serve as a plumb line—the thing you measure every idea against. If a past event or future idea doesn't fit your mission statement, then it needs to be either tweaked or removed. I realize this may come across as harsh or lacking grace, but standard-setting is biblical. I have witnessed a stark difference in participation and fruit when women's ministry plans are prayerful, focused, and organized compared to when they are not.

Even when you've covered the decision and every step with prayer, there's a very strong possibility you'll encounter opposition to any changes you make. Expect to encounter some pushback, and then you won't be blindsided when it comes. Prayer and sound planning will help minimize the opposition, but even so, some of your women won't like anyone messing with an event, tradition, or element they dearly love. It may feel as if those against the change far outnumber those who are for the change, but feelings can be deceiving.

Kriegel and Brandt state, "Overcoming resistance is about neutralizing negativity."[5] It's up to you and your team to paint a picture of what's possible. What will the benefits of this change be? Will you reach more women in your community? Will you have the funds to invest in a new event or project your women desire? What's the impact of leaving things the same?

Here are some tactics for responding to critics:

1. A simple "Thank you for sharing your concerns" may be enough to appease some of your women who are vocally opposed to the changes.
2. It can be helpful to explain the reasoning behind the changes at your fall kickoff or start to Bible study. For example: "We're excited about how this change will allow working women in our church to participate," or "Our team has been praying about how we can better reach out to women in the community, and we're excited to add more opportunities for outreach to our women's ministry calendar this year."
3. Pause before you respond. I have to be very careful when I am confident in God's leading that I don't bulldoze the naysayers. To keep myself from saying things I'll have to apologize for later, I have a twenty-four-hour rule. I make myself wait for twenty-four hours before I respond to criticism. Usually, that's enough time for me to work through my emotions and reply in a more Christlike manner. My husband is also a great sounding board, and I almost always ask him to read any written communication before I send it. Writing also helps me to work through my thoughts. I never enter a recipient's email address when I'm typing up an email, though, as I know there's always the chance I'll hit the wrong button and send it accidentally before it's ready.

Some women may decide that, rather than adapt to the changes you and your team have made, they will stop participating. Try not to take it personally. Sometimes God will remove the opposition so the ministry can move forward. I know that sounds harsh and not very sympathetic, but I've been the recipient of such an event. You may remember I mentioned a team we had to rebuild from the ground up; the women who opposed the changes we were going to make decided to leave the team. It would have been much easier to give in rather than to stand firm and accept their resignations.

They were not happy with me, and they made their feelings known. I cried in frustration behind closed doors, but I stood firm. Were it not for God's crystal-clear calling, godly wisdom from a mentor, and scriptural confirmation, I would have walked away. Obedience amid change can be hard.

Obedience amid change can be hard.

Is it worth it? Yes! Absolutely, yes. Kriegel and Brandt insist, "getting rid of a sacred cow will free up time, energy, and resources so you can tackle more valuable work."[6] Not only will God grow and refine our faith in Him but change can provide the opportunity to reach women who are not coming. Let's bring those women that are sitting on the sidelines into the game. Let's invite them to live a life where Jesus is everything.

Consider what will happen if you don't make the changes God has prompted you or your team to make. Are those consequences you can live with?

Reflection Questions

1. Make a list of women's ministry practices, events, and activities in your church that could be considered sacred cows. If you're stuck, consider what would cause an outcry if your team stopped doing it.

2. How do you sense God is prompting your team to respond to these sacred cows?

3. What did you find most encouraging or challenging in this chapter?

Praying Through the Process

Lord, give us discernment when it comes to events that are a tradition in our women's ministry. Help us to know when we've strayed from Your purpose. Give us the insight to make any necessary changes. Prepare the hearts of our women as we seek to do Your will. Amen.

Women's Ministry Health Assessment

First, answer the questions. Be specific. Your answers should reflect how and why, not just a yes or no.

Then rate each area on a scale from 1 to 10.

1 = None / Lacking greatly
5 = Fair / Some
10 = Off the charts / No need for improvement

1. **Spiritual growth.** Health Rating ______
   Describe several examples of unbelievers who have come into a relationship with Christ through your ministry. If you can't think of any, how often do you think this happens in your ministry? Describe examples of how women are engaging in discipleship and growing spiritually. If you can't think of any, what would it look like if you observed this in your ministry? List examples of how women are increasingly spending time in prayer, God's Word, and service.

2. **Reputation.** Health Rating ______
   How would you describe the overall sentiment toward the women's ministry in your church? What is your ministry's reputation? Ask some women outside of your leadership team. Ask the pastoral staff. Are you viewed as a clique? Exclusive? Welcoming? Warm?

3. **Leadership.** Health Rating ______

   List several examples of ways you are developing new leaders. Describe your plan to seek them out among the women in your church. List examples that show whether you have the same core group of women leading everything or are open to new faces in your leadership circle.

4. **Volunteers.** Health Rating ______

   How would you describe the strength of your volunteer teams? What type of response do you receive when you ask for volunteers? Describe the attitude of your volunteers. Are they compassionate and committed or weary and stale?

5. **Attendance.** Health Rating ______

   What do your numbers tell you? Make a list of events that have a strong, solid turnout and those events and activities that are struggling. Keep in mind that a strong turnout is not equivalent to a gold star from God. Some of the best-attended events can be lacking in direction or mission.

6. **Mission.** Health Rating ______

   What is the focus of your women's ministry? Describe how your women's ministry fulfills its mission or purpose. Explain how your church would be at a loss if your women's ministry ceased to exist.

7. **Outreach.** Health Rating ______

   List ways in which your events and activities include women from outside of the church. Explain how your team utilizes the women's ministry as a bridge, encouraging women to attend worship and serve as part of the church body.

Finally, total up your health ratings: ______

Scores	Assessment
55–70	Congratulations, your ministry is healthy! If you haven't asked your pastoral staff to complete the assessment, please consider doing so to make certain you haven't missed any signs or symptoms that need attention.
30–54	Looks like your ministry is in fair to good health. Where can you make some changes to push your ministry into the healthy zone? Be quick to address areas that rated a 4 or lower.
15–29	You need to make a consult with the Great Physician. It appears you may be struggling with some chronic issues. Let's nip things in the bud and create a plan to address areas that scored below a 4. You may want to tackle a different area each month at your team meeting.
0–14	Your ministry is showing signs and symptoms that need to be addressed immediately. Work together to come up with a plan to address the most chronic needs first. God is in the restoration business; let's pray and seek wise counsel to restore your ministry's health.

This exercise is not designed to make you or your team feel bad but to shine a light on areas of your ministry that need some extra attention and to celebrate those areas in which your team excels.

Let's celebrate what we do well and embrace the growth opportunities God reveals to us. None of us is perfect, and I don't expect any ministry to score a perfect 70. It's easy to lose sight of the greater picture in the midst of planning events and activities. We can become so focused on our women having fun that we miss opportunities to encourage spiritual growth, discipleship, and service. Take this opportunity to see the bigger picture and fuel change where it is needed.

Consider making this assessment an annual process, always working toward creating a healthier ministry.

Conclusion

It's time to put on your apron and get to work developing a menu of women's ministry events and activities that will invite your women to "Taste and see that the Lord is good [and take] refuge in him" (Ps. 34:8). A women's ministry calendar filled with purposefully, prayerfully planned events will help your women develop a hunger for God and His Word. You've got the tools you need to move forward with confidence.

Not sure where to start?

- Spend some time reviewing the Scripture verses that support women's ministry (Titus 2:3–5; Acts 2:42; and Matt. 28:19–20).
- Reread the accounts of women God used in Scripture to support and grow His kingdom, such as Priscilla, Mary, and Hannah. God needs women to be prayer warriors, caregivers, theologians, evangelists, and disciple-makers. With your guidance and encouragement, the women in your church will embrace and fulfill these roles. What a blessing they will be to your church and future generations.

After you've spent some time reflecting on God's Word:

- Go back to the beginning of this book and identify any part of your women's ministry foundation that needs to be strengthened. Do you need to add a team member or two? Do you need to meet with your pastor or take a closer look at the women you're serving? Do you need to create a mission statement?

- Look back at the pages you've highlighted. Spend time in prayer asking God for wisdom about what your team and the women in your church need.

Next, make plans to review your ministry calendar with your team:

- Add a Bible study, if needed.
- Note what type of women's ministry events make up your current calendar (discipleship practices, biblical encouragement, practical skills, service, and fellowship) and close any gaps.

Finally, complete the women's ministry health assessment to identify any areas that need to be addressed.

It can be so easy to lose focus on what's most important about women's ministry. We can get distracted by fancy decor, creative event ideas on social media, and what the women's ministry team across town is offering. Focusing on the essentials of women's ministry will keep you and your team concentrated on the task God's given you. What is that task? Paul's wise counsel to his mentee, Timothy, holds true for us too. God "wants all people to be saved and to come to a knowledge of the truth. For there is one God and one mediator between God and mankind, the man Christ Jesus, who gave himself as a ransom for all people" (1 Tim. 2:4–6). Your women need Jesus. May everything you do point them to Him.

A Prayer for Leaders

Father,

I thank You for the leader reading this book. I thank You for the church in which she serves. I pray You'll provide the specific things she needs to share the gospel with the women in her church and community.

I ask You to send women to serve alongside her. Give her discernment to know which women she should ask to serve in leadership roles.

Hold her up when she is discouraged. Please give her glimpses of the fruit of her labor to spur her on.

Lord, please protect her time in Your Word. Help her to know and love You more.

May all that she does glorify You.

Amen.

For this reason, since the day we heard about you, we have not stopped praying for you. We continually ask God to fill you with the knowledge of his will through all the wisdom and understanding that the Spirit gives, so that you may live a life worthy of the Lord and please him in every way: bearing fruit in every good work, growing in the knowledge of God, being strengthened with all power according to his glorious might so that you may have great endurance and patience, and giving joyful thanks to the Father, who has qualified you to share in the inheritance of his holy people in the kingdom of light. (Col. 1:9–12)

Acknowledgments

Kim, Lois, Becki, and Susan, you are mighty prayer warriors, and I thank you for encouraging me to step into that very first women's ministry director position. Thank you for seeing God's next steps when I could not see them myself.

To the women's ministry team members I've served alongside: Thank you for praying with me and for me. You helped me to be a better leader. You showed me how to serve with grace and love. Thank you for brainstorming with me and for your willingness to try new things. It's been my greatest joy to love the women in each church with you.

To the leaders in the Women's Ministry Toolbox Community: You are the reason this book exists. Thank you for wanting more for the women in your churches and for the many ways you share Jesus with the women in your churches. Thank you for the sweet notes of encouragement so many of you have sent over the years, and for using the resources I share. Our Facebook group is one of the best and most encouraging places on the internet!

To my beta team readers: Becki, Dee, Rene, and Angie. Thank you for your feedback, encouragement, and suggestions. You've helped to make this book better.

To my book prayer team members and launch team: Your prayers and excitement for this project kept me moving forward.

To my mom, Becki, and my sisters, Kristy and Katy: Thank you for praying for me and encouraging me through this process. Your support and feedback have meant so much.

To my agent, Bob Hostetler: Thank you for taking a second chance on me. Your prayers and guidance have been greatly appreciated.

To my editor, Eddie LaRow: Thank you for seeing the need for this book and for believing that women's ministry matters.

To the team at Baker Publishing—Carrie Weston, Eileen Hanson, Jessica English, and Lindsey Spoolstra: Thank you for taking my words and ideas and crafting them into this beautiful book. Because of your labor, many more leaders will have the essential ingredients they need to build and sustain a thriving women's ministry program.

I am most thankful for my Lord and Savior, who saw it fit to create a heart in me for women's ministry. I am humbled and grateful for the opportunities You give me to share Your Word and the gospel with other women.

Notes

Introduction

1. Warren W. Wiersbe, *The Wiersbe Bible Commentary: The Complete Old Testament in One Volume* (David C Cook, 2007), 915.

Chapter 1 Why Women's Ministry Matters

1. Gallup, "Religion," Gallup, accessed March 25, 2025, https://news.gallup.com/poll/1690/Religion.aspx.

2. Center for Bible Engagement (CBE), "Producing Research & Resources That Lead to Life Transformation," CBE, accessed August 29, 2024, https://www.centerforbibleengagement.org/research.

3. Tracy Munsil, "Biblical Worldview Among U.S. Adults Drops 33% Since Start of COVID-19 Pandemic," Arizona Christian University, February 28, 2023, www.arizonachristian.edu/2023/02/28/biblical-worldview-among-u-s-adults-drops-33-since-start-of-covid-19-pandemic/.

4. Jeffery Fulks et al., "State of the Bible USA 2024," American Bible Society, pdf, accessed March 12, 2025, https://1s712.americanbible.org/state-of-the-bible/stateofthebible/State_of_the_bible-2024.pdf.

5. Jean M. Twenge, *Generations: The Real Differences Between Gen Z, Millennials, Gen X, Boomers, and Silents—and What They Mean for America's Future* (Atria Books, 2023), 345.

6. Twenge, *Generations*, 347, 349.

7. Twenge, *Generations*, 363, 364.

8. Abigail Shrier, *Bad Therapy: Why the Kids Aren't Growing Up* (Sentinel, 2024), 33.

9. Twenge, *Generations*, 377.

10. Twenge, *Generations*, 396.

11. Shrier, *Bad Therapy*, 17.

12. Twenge, *Generations*, 396, 416.

13. Barna, "Over Half of Gen Z Teens Feel Motivated to Learn More About Jesus," Barna Group, February 1, 2023, www.barna.com/research/teens-and-jesus/.

14. Barna Group and Impact 360, *Gen Z: The Culture, Beliefs and Motivations Shaping the Next Generation* (Barna Group, 2018), 26.

15. Kyle Richter and Patrick Miller, "5 Reasons Gen Z Is Primed for Spiritual Renewal," TGC, October 9, 2023, www.thegospelcoalition.org/article/gen-z-primed-spiritual-renewal/.
16. Twenge, *Generations*, 255, 259, 278–79, 293.
17. Twenge, *Generations*, 330, 339, 341.
18. Twenge, *Generations*, 301, 302.
19. Twenge, *Generations*, 150, 157.
20. Twenge, *Generations*, 160, 166, 217.
21. Twenge, *Generations*, 76, 85, 84.
22. Twenge, *Generations*, 89, 91, 93.
23. Twenge, *Generations*, 136.
24. Twenge, *Generations*, 2.

Chapter 2 Building a Firm Foundation for a Ministry That Lasts

1. G. William Schweer, "Evangelism," ed. Chad Brand et al., *Holman Illustrated Bible Dictionary* (Holman Bible Publishers, 2003), 518.

Chapter 3 Assembling and Leading a Strong Ministry Team

1. Got Questions, "What Should We Learn from the Account of Paul and Barnabas?," Got Questions Ministries, accessed November 11, 2024, www.gotquestions.org/Paul-and-Barnabas.html.

Chapter 4 Discipleship Pathways

1. Warren W. Wiersbe, *The Wiersbe Bible Commentary: The Complete New Testament in One Volume* (David C Cook, 2007), 782.
2. CBE, "Producing Research & Resources."
3. CBE, "Producing Research & Resources."
4. Kandi Gallaty, *Disciple Her: Using the Word, Work, & Wonder of God to Invest in Women* (B&H, 2019), 32.
5. Melissa B. Kruger, *Growing Together: Taking Mentoring Beyond Small Talk and Prayer Requests* (Crossway, 2020), 19.
6. Robby Gallaty, *MARCS of a Disciple: A Biblical Guide for Gauging Spiritual Growth* (Replicate Resources, 2016), xx.
7. Nancy DeMoss Wolgemuth, *Adorned: Living Out the Beauty of the Gospel Together* (Moody, 2017), 75.

Chapter 6 Cultivating Community and Crushing Cliques

1. US Department of Health and Human Services (HHS), "New Surgeon General Advisory Raises Alarm About the Devastating Impact of the Epidemic of Loneliness and Isolation in the United States," May 3, 2023, www.hhs.gov/about/news/2023/05/03/new-surgeon-general-advisory-raises-alarm-about-devastating-impact-epidemic-loneliness-isolation-united-states.html.
2. HHS, "New Surgeon General Advisory Raises Alarm."
3. *Cambridge Dictionary*, "clique," accessed November 12, 2025, https://dictionary.cambridge.org/us/dictionary/english/clique.
4. Glenna Marshall, *Everyday Faithfulness: The Beauty of Ordinary Perseverance in a Demanding World* (Crossway, 2020), 21.

5. Marshall, *Everyday Faithfulness*, 152.
6. Kruger, *Growing Together*, 61.
7. Thom S. Rainer, *Becoming a Welcoming Church* (B&H, 2018), 2–3.
8. Rainer, *Becoming a Welcoming Church*, 8.

Chapter 7 Engaging in Missions, Service Projects, and Evangelism

1. Bob Compton, "Mission(s)," *Holman Illustrated Bible Dictionary*, 1140.
2. G. William Schweer, "Evangelism," *Holman Illustrated Bible Dictionary*, 518.
3. Schweer, "Evangelism," *Holman Illustrated Bible Dictionary*, 518.
4. Steven Corbett and Brian Fikkert, *When Helping Hurts: How to Alleviate Poverty Without Hurting the Poor . . . and Yourself*, new edition (Moody, 2012), 27.
5. Corbett and Fikkert, *When Helping Hurts*, 99.

Chapter 8 Communicating Clearly

1. Kathi Kruse, "Rule of 7: How Social Media Crushes Old School Marketing," Kruse Control Inc, January 4, 2024, www.krusecontrolinc.com/rule-of-7-how-social-media-crushes-old-school-marketing-2024/.

Chapter 9 Navigating Change and Addressing Sacred Cows

1. Robert Kriegel and David Brandt, *Sacred Cows Make the Best Burgers: Developing Change-Driving People and Organizations* (Warner Books, 1996), 1.
2. Thom S. Rainer, "15 Common Sacred Cows in Churches," *Church Answers* (blog), August 27, 2018, https://churchanswers.com/blog/15-common-sacred-cows-churches/.
3. Kriegel and Brandt, *Sacred Cows*, 181.
4. Kriegel and Brandt, *Sacred Cows*, 212.
5. Kriegel and Brandt, *Sacred Cows*, 234.
6. Kriegel and Brandt, *Sacred Cows*, 146.

Janell Wood

CYNDEE OWNBEY mentors thousands of women's ministry leaders through her Women's Ministry Toolbox website, Facebook group, and podcast. With over twenty-five years of experience serving women in five churches, Cyndee offers a practical, relatable perspective rooted in Scripture. She enjoys training leaders and teaching at women's events and conferences, equipping women to lead with confidence and clarity. Cyndee is currently completing her MA in ministry to women at Southeastern Baptist Theological Seminary and serves on the women's ministry team at her local church in Concord, North Carolina. She and her husband are blessed to have two adult sons and two wonderful daughters-in-law. When they are not spending time with family, you might find them traveling or relaxing at the beach. In her free time, Cyndee loves reading, trying new recipes, and taking long walks while listening to her favorite podcasts.

CONNECT WITH CYNDEE:

WomensMinistryToolbox.com

@WomensMinistryToolbox

@WomensMinistryToolbox

@WomensMinistryToolbox